Mastering Kotlin

Mastering Kotlin helps readers quickly understand core concepts and then move on to practical projects using the Kotlin programming language.

Back in the day, Java was the de facto choice for creating Android apps. However, since Google announced Kotlin as the new language of choice for building Android applications, developers haven't looked back.

Kotlin is a general-purpose, statically typed, open source programming language that runs on Java Virtual Machines. It can be called a Java replacement; however, the Kotlin syntax isn't blindly identical to that of Java. Sure, Kotlin can work with Java, and owing to its intuitiveness, it can also enhance overall productivity and efficiency, but it is not a Java clone.

Kotlin differs from Java in that it has assertive interfaces that help determine variables and expressions classes, even if they're not defined. Kotlin is a beautiful alternative for modifying and identifying faults because it has a familiar and straightforward syntax and programming structure. It comes with a sophisticated compiler that can track automatic casts, allowing verification durations to be more efficient. Kotlin also has simple signals that may be interpreted without any need for set parameters. And Kotlin is easy to set up: all you need is a Kotlin component for Android Studio.

Kotlin developers are in high demand. As a Kotlin developer, you'll be able to pursue a variety of career routes, spanning fields such as mobile app dev, game dev, game design, and even software development. Many well-known brands use Kotlin in their software and projects. Naturally, it is a good idea to learn Kotlin, and this is where *Mastering Kotlin* can be the right manual for you!

With *Mastering Kotlin*, learning Kotlin becomes an easy task, and learners can use their skills to create innovative Kotlin apps.

The *Mastering Computer Science* series is edited by Sufyan bin Uzayr, a writer and educator with over a decade of experience in the computing field.

Mastering Computer Science
Series Editor: Sufyan bin Uzayr

Mastering Kotlin: A Beginner's Guide
Divya Sachdeva, Faruq KC, and Aruqqa Khateib

Mastering KDE: A Beginner's Guide
Jaskiran Kaur, Mathew Rooney, and Shahryar Raz

Mastering GNOME: A Beginner's Guide
Jaskiran Kaur, Mathew Rooney, and Reza Nafim

Mastering Flutter: A Beginner's Guide
Divya Sachdeva, NT Ozman, and Reza Nafim

Mastering Visual Studio Code: A Beginner's Guide
Jaskiran Kaur, D Nikitenko, and Mathew Rooney

Mastering Ubuntu: A Beginner's Guide
Jaskiran Kaur, Rubina Salafey, and Shahryar Raz

For more information about this series, please visit: https://www.routledge
.com/Mastering-Computer-Science/book-series/MCS

The "Mastering Computer Science" series of books are authored by the Zeba Academy team members, led by Sufyan bin Uzayr.

Zeba Academy is an EdTech venture that develops courses and content for learners primarily in STEM fields, and offers education consulting to Universities and Institutions worldwide. For more info, please visit https://zeba.academy.

Mastering Kotlin
A Beginner's Guide

Edited by
Sufyan bin Uzayr

CRC Press
Taylor & Francis Group
Boca Raton London New York

CRC Press is an imprint of the
Taylor & Francis Group, an **informa** business

First Edition published 2023
by CRC Press
6000 Broken Sound Parkway NW, Suite 300, Boca Raton, FL 33487-2742

and by CRC Press
2 Park Square, Milton Park, Abingdon, Oxon, OX14 4RN

CRC Press is an imprint of Taylor & Francis Group, LLC

© 2023 Sufyan bin Uzayr

Library of Congress Cataloging-in-Publication Data

Names: Bin Uzayr, Sufyan, editor.
Title: Mastering Kotlin : a beginner's guide / edited by Sufyan bin Uzayr.
Description: First edition. | Boca Raton : CRC Press, 2023. |
Series: Mastering computer science | Includes bibliographical references and index.
Identifiers: LCCN 2022021392 (print) | LCCN 2022021393 (ebook) | ISBN 9781032318950 (hardback) | ISBN 9781032318851 (paperback) | ISBN 9781003311904 (ebook)
Subjects: LCSH: Android (Electronic resource) | Kotlin (Computer program language) | Application software--Development. | Mobile apps--Development. | Java (Computer program language)
Classification: LCC QA76.73.K68 M37 2023 (print) | LCC QA76.73.K68 (ebook) | DDC 005.4/45--dc23/eng/20220810
LC record available at https://lccn.loc.gov/2022021392
LC ebook record available at https://lccn.loc.gov/2022021393

ISBN: 9781032318950 (hbk)
ISBN: 9781032318851 (pbk)
ISBN: 9781003311904 (ebk)

DOI: 10.1201/9781003311904

Typeset in Minion
by KnowledgeWorks Global Ltd.

Contents

Preface

The *Mastering Computer Science* series covers a wide range of topics, spanning programming languages as well as modern-day technologies and frameworks. The series has a special focus on beginner-level content, and is presented in an easy-to-understand manner, comprising:

- Crystal-clear text, spanning various topics sorted by relevance,

- A special focus on practical exercises, with numerous code samples and programs,

- A guided approach to programming, with step-by-step tutorials for the absolute beginners,

- Keen emphasis on real-world utility of skills, thereby cutting the redundant and seldom-used concepts and focusing instead on the industry-prevalent coding paradigm, and

- A wide range of references and resources to help both beginner and intermediate-level developers gain the most out of the books.

The *Mastering Computer Science* series of books start from the core concepts, and then quickly move on to industry-standard coding practices, to help learners gain efficient and crucial skills in as little time as possible. The books assume no prior knowledge of coding, so even absolute newbie coders can benefit from this series.

The *Mastering Computer Science* series is edited by Sufyan bin Uzayr, a writer and educator with more than a decade of experience in the computing field.

About the Author

Sufyan bin Uzayr is a writer, coder, and entrepreneur with over a decade of experience in the industry. He has authored several books in the past, pertaining to a diverse range of topics, ranging from History to Computers/IT.

Sufyan is the Director of Parakozm, a multinational IT company specializing in EdTech solutions. He also runs Zeba Academy, an online learning and teaching vertical with a focus on STEM fields.

Sufyan specializes in a wide variety of technologies such as JavaScript, Dart, WordPress, Drupal, Linux, and Python. He holds multiple degrees, including ones in Management, IT, Literature, and Political Science.

Sufyan is a digital nomad, dividing his time between four countries. He has lived and taught in universities and educational institutions around the globe. Sufyan takes a keen interest in technology, politics, literature, history, and sports, and in his spare time, he enjoys teaching coding and English to young students.

Learn more at sufyanism.com.

CHAPTER 1

Getting Started

IN THIS CHAPTER

➤ Introduction

➤ Environment setup

➤ Data types, variables, and operators

➤ Type conversion

➤ Standard input/output

Kotlin is a free and open-source programming language that can execute the Java Virtual Machine (JVM). The language can operate on a variety of systems.

It is a language that blends Object-Oriented Programming (OOP) with functional programming in an open, self-contained, and separate platform.

Example:

```kotlin
fun main()
{
    println("Hello Everyone");
}
```

DOI: 10.1201/9781003311904-1

1

HISTORY OF KOTLIN

The following are significant landmarks in Kotlin's history:

- Kotlin v1.0 was released in 2016.

- Google made an announcement in 2017 about first-class Kotlin support in Android.

- Kotlin v1.3 was released in 2018, adding coroutines for asynchronous programming.

- Google chose Kotlin as their preferred programming language for Android app developers in 2019.

FEATURES OF KOTLIN

The following are major Kotlin features:

- Provides Reduced Coding.

- Kotlin uses the JVM, which combines the benefits of OOP with functional programming.

- Provides quick compilation.

- Kotlin supports a wide range of extension functions without code modifications.

- Kotlin code may be written using an IDE or the command-line interface.

- Smart feature casting reduces application expenses, while increasing application speed or performance.

KOTLIN'S KEY CHARACTERISTICS

- **Statically typed:** A programming language feature that implies the type of every variable and expression is known at compile time. It is a statically typed language; it does not need us to define every variable declared.

- **Data Classes:** In Kotlin, Data Classes lead to the auto-generation of boilerplate code such as equals, hashCode, function toString(), getters/setters, and much more.

Consider the following scenario:

```
class Books {
    private String titles;
    private Author authors;
    public String getTitle()
    {
        return titles;
    }
    public void setTitle(String titles)
    {
        this.titles = titles;
    }
    public Author getAuthor()
    {
        return authors;
    }
    public void setAuthor(Author authors)
    {
        this.authors = authors;
    }
}
```

However, in Kotlin, the above class is defined in a single line:

```
/* Kotlin Code */
data class Book(var titles:String, var authors:Author)
```

- **Concise:** It significantly decreases the amount of unnecessary code written in other object-oriented programming languages.

- **Safe:** It is protected from the most obnoxious and aggravating NullPointerExceptions since it supports nullability as part of its system.

By default, every variable in Kotlin is non-null.

```
String s = "Hello Everyone"    // Non-null
```

When we assign a null value, we get a build time error. So,

```
s = null                    // compile-time error
```

To assign a null value to a string, it must first be declared nullable.

```
String nullableStr? = null // compiles successfully
```

- **Interoperability with Java:** Because Kotlin runs on the JVM, it is entirely compatible with Java. We can efficiently utilize java code from Kotlin and Kotlin code from Java.

- **Functional and object-oriented capabilities:** Kotlin features many helpful techniques, including higher-order functions, lambda expressions, operator overloading, lazy evaluation, operator overloading, and many others.

A higher-order function receives a function as an argument, returns a function, or does both.

Higher-order function illustration:

```
fun myFun(company: String,product: String, fn:
(String,String) -> String): Unit {
    val results = fn(company,product)
    println(results)
}

fun main(args: Array){
    val fn:(String,String)->String={org,portal->"$org
develops $portal"}
    myFun("Kotlin","JetBrain",fn)
}
```

- **Smart Cast:** It explicitly typecasts immutable values and automatically inserts the value in its safe cast.

    A compilation error will be generated if we attempt to access a nullable type of String (String? = "BYEBYE") without using the safe cast.

```
fun main(args: Array){
    var string: String? = "BYEBYE"
        print(string.length)          // compile time
error
    }
}

fun main(args: Array){
    var string: String? = "BYEBYE"
    if(string != null) {              // smart cast
        print(string.length)
    }
}
```

- **Compilation time:** It has a faster compilation time and more excellent performance.

    It is tool-friendly, with excellent tooling support. Kotlin may use any Java IDEs, including IntelliJ IDEA, Eclipse, and Android Studio. Kotlin programs may also execute Kotlin programs from the command line.

Kotlin programming language has the following advantages:

- **It is simple to learn:** Basic is almost identical to Java. If we've worked with Java before, we'll be up and running in no time.

- **Kotlin is platform-agnostic:** Because all Java IDEs support Kotlin, we may develop our programs and run them on any system that promotes JVM.

- It's far more secure than Java.

- It enables Java frameworks and libraries in new Kotlin projects by utilizing complex frameworks without updating the entire project in Java.

HOW KOTLIN MULTIPLATFORM FUNCTIONS

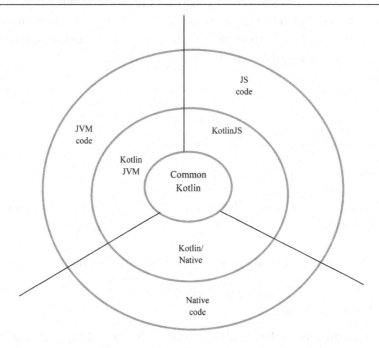

Multiplatform in Kotlin.

- The language, essential libraries, and basic tools are all included in Common Kotlin. Code written in common Kotlin runs on all platforms.

- We may reuse multiplatform logic in standard and platform-specific code with Kotlin Multiplatform libraries.

- Platform-specific Kotlin versions should use for interoperability. Platform-specific Kotlin versions (Kotlin/JVM, Kotlin/JS, and Kotlin/Native) provide language extensions and platform-specific libraries and tools.

- We may access the platform's native code (JVM, JS, and Native) and use all native features through these platforms.

KOTLIN'S ARCHITECTURE

A well-designed architecture is essential for an application to scale its features and match the end user base's expectations. Kotlin has its own unique and exclusive architecture for allocating memory and producing high-quality results for developers and end users.

Kotlin's coroutines and classes construct the core so that less boilerplate code is produced, performance is increased, and efficiency is reinforced. The Kotlin compiler can behave differently in several situations, particularly when earmarking distinct types of languages.

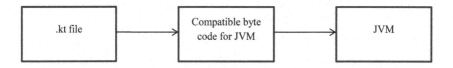

Architecture in Kotlin.

The architectural design clearly shows that code execution takes three simple phases.

- The first step is to add a ".kt" or Kotlin file to the compiler.

- The code is then converted into bytecode by the Kotlin compiler in the second stage.

- The bytecode is then loaded into the JVM and executed by the JVM in the third stage.

When a pair of bytecoded files run on the JVM, they initiate mutual communication, which is how the Kotlin feature known as interoperability for Java came to be.

Kotlin to JavaScript transformation occurs when Kotlin targets JavaScript.

When JavaScript is selected as the target, any Kotlin code part of the library that sails Kotlin is then spilled with JavaScript. The Java Development Kit (JDK) or any java library used, on the other hand, is not included.

A non-Kotlin file is not considered during this process. While aiming toward JavaScript, the Kotlin compiler converts the kt file into ES5.1 to output consistent JavaScript code. The Kotlin compiler strives for optimal output size, interoperability with existing modules, standard library functionality, and JavaScript readable output.

The discussion has shown that Kotlin compilers may produce more efficient, competent, and independent code, resulting in a high-performing software product.

KOTLIN VS. JAVA

Key features:

- Kotlin mixes object-oriented and functional programming capabilities, whereas Java is confined to object-oriented programming.

- Kotlin allows users to write their extension functions, but Java does not.

- Implicit conversions are not available in Kotlin; however, they are supported in Java.

- In Kotlin, there are no null variables or objects; yet, null variables and objects are part of the Java programming language.

- Kotlin does not support static members, unlike Java does.

- Variables of a primitive type in Kotlin are objects, but variables of a primitive type in Java are not.

- Kotlin supports Lambda Expression, although Java does not.

- Variable data type specifications are not required in Kotlin, although needed in Java.

- Variable data type definitions are not required in Kotlin, although they are necessary for Java.

- Semicolons are not required in Kotlin programs, although they are required in Java programs.

- Language scripting features enable us to utilize Kotlin directly in Gradle build scripts, whereas Java does not support language scripting.

Here are the distinctions between Kotlin and Java:

Kotlin	Java
Users can develop extension functions in Kotlin.	Java does not support extension functions.
For data classes, Kotlin does not necessitate a lot of effort.	To create classes, Java developers must write and construct many components.
Implicit conversions are not available in Kotlin.	Java allows for implicit conversions.
In Kotlin, there are no null variables or objects.	The Java programming language has null variables and objects.
Kotlin is a computer language that incorporates object-oriented and functional programming elements.	Java is only capable of object-oriented programming.
Static members are not supported in Kotlin.	Java makes use of static members.
Objects are variables of a primitive type.	Primitive type variables are not objects.
We can have one or more secondary constructors in Kotlin.	Secondary constructors are not allowed in Java. It can, however, have many constructors.
The Kotlin string template also supports expressions.	Java strings, unlike Kotlin, do not support expressions.
Kotlin code is much easier to deploy.	Java programming is challenging to deploy.
Semicolons are not required in Kotlin programming.	A semicolon is required in a Java application.
Coroutines are concurrency design patterns in Kotlin that may use to simplify coding.	Java takes advantage of two coroutine options: (1) Rx Java and (2) Project loom.
There are no wildcard types in Kotlin.	Java has a wildcard feature.
Kotlin's system features built-in null safety.	NullPonter Exception is primarily responsible for Java and Android development.
In Kotlin, the smart cast functionality is accessible.	Java does not support the smart cast capability.

(Continued)

Kotlin	Java
Variable data type specifications are not required in Kotlin.	Variable data type specifications are required in Java.
Kotlin supports lambda expression.	Java does not support lambda expression.
Kotlin includes the Lazy-Loading functionality.	Java does not support this functionality.
Kotlin has language scripting capabilities; we may use it directly in our Gradle build scripts.	Java does not support language scripting.
Kotlin supports contemporary programming notions like delegates, extensions, and higher-order functions.	Java supports the OOP's paradigm.
The annual pay range for "Kotlin" is around $107,275 for Software engineers to $121,034 for Android Developers.	The annual compensation for a java developer is $104,793.

KOTLIN MULTIPLATFORM IN MOBILE

Kotlin Multiplatform Mobile (KMM) is an SDK that makes it easier to create cross-platform mobile applications. With KMM, we can share standard code between iOS and Android apps while writing platform-specific code only when it is required. For example, developing a native user interface (UI) or working with platform-specific APIs.

Begin with Kotlin Multiplatform Mobile
Platforms That Are Supported
KMM is compatible with the following mobile targets:

- Applications and libraries for Android.

- Android NDK supports ARM32 and ARM64 processors.

- Apple iOS on ARM64 (iPhone 5s and later), ARM32 (previous models), and desktop simulators on Intel-based and Apple Silicon platforms.

- Apple watchOS is available on ARM64 (Apple Watch Series 4 and later) and ARM32 (previous versions) platforms and desktop simulators on Intel-based and Apple Silicon systems.

- KMM is built on the Kotlin Multiplatform technology, which supports various platforms such as JavaScript, Linux, WebAssembly, etc.

Kotlin for Server-Side

Kotlin is an excellent choice for designing server-side apps since it allows us to create expressive and straightforward code while remaining fully compatible with current Java-based technology stacks and having a short learning curve:

- **Expressivity:** Kotlin's novel language featured, including type-safe constructors and delegated properties, aid in creating strong and easy-to-use abstractions.

- **Scalability:** Kotlin's support for coroutines aids in the development of server-side applications that scale to enormous numbers of clients while using little hardware.

- **Interoperability:** Kotlin is completely interoperable with all Java-based frameworks, allowing us to continue on our existing technology stack while benefiting from a more contemporary language.

- **Transfer:** Kotlin facilitates the incremental, step-by-step migration of huge Java codebases to Kotlin. We may begin developing new code in Kotlin while still maintaining existing sections of our system in Java.

- **Tooling:** In addition to excellent IDE support with general, Kotlin provides framework-specific tooling (for example, Spring) in the IntelliJ IDEA Ultimate plugin.

- **Learning Curve:** Getting started with Kotlin is relatively simple for a Java developer. The Kotlin plugin's automatic Java to Kotlin converter aids in the initial phases. Kotlin Koans walk us through the language's essential features with a series of interactive activities.

Kotlin Frameworks for Server-Side Development

- Spring begins with version 5.0, using Kotlin language capabilities to provide more succinct APIs. The online project generator enables us to create a new Kotlin project easily.

- Vert.x, a framework for developing reactive Web applications on the JVM, has extensive documentation and specialized support for Kotlin.

- Ktor is a JetBrains framework for developing Web apps in Kotlin that uses coroutines for high scalability and provides an easy-to-use and idiomatic API.

- kotlinx.html is a DSL for creating HTML in a Web application. It's an excellent alternative to classic templating technologies like JSP and FreeMarker.

- Micronaut is a full-stack, contemporary, JVM-based framework for developing modular, testable microservice, and serverless applications. It has a plethora of useful built-in functions.

- http4k is a small-footprint functional toolkit for Kotlin HTTP applications built entirely in Kotlin. The library is based on Twitter's "Our Server as a Function" and depicts HTTP Servers and Clients as simple Kotlin functions combined.

- Javalin is a Kotlin and Java web framework that supports WebSockets, HTTP2, and async requests.

- Direct JDBC access, JPA, and the use of NoSQL databases via Java drivers are all alternatives for persistence. The kotlin-jpa compiler plugin for JPA adjusts Kotlin-compiled classes to the framework's specifications.

Using Kotlin to Deploy Server-Side Apps
Kotlin apps may run on any host that supports Java Web applications, such as Amazon Web Services, Google Cloud Platform, etc.

Kotlin for Android

- Since Google I/O in 2019, Android mobile development has become Kotlin-first.

- When we use Kotlin for Android development, we get less code and better readability. Spend less time creating code and more time attempting to comprehend the code of others.

- Language and environment that is mature. Since its inception in 2011, Kotlin has evolved not just as a language but also as a complete ecosystem with sophisticated tools. It is now fully integrated into Android Studio and is actively utilized by numerous businesses to create Android applications.

- Support for Kotlin in Android Jetpack and other libraries. KTX extensions extend current Android libraries with Kotlin language features such as coroutines, extension functions, lambdas, and named arguments.

- Java interoperability. We may utilize Kotlin alongside Java in our apps without moving all of our code to Kotlin.

- Multiplatform development is supported. Kotlin may use it to create Android and iOS, backend, and web apps. Make use of the advantages of sharing the common code throughout platforms.

- Code security. Less code and improved readability result in fewer mistakes. The remaining errors are detected by the Kotlin compiler, rendering the code safe.

- Learning is simple. Kotlin is a relatively simple language to learn, especially for Java developers.

- A large community. The Kotlin community, which is growing worldwide, has given it a lot of support and numerous contributions. According to Google, Kotlin is used by more than 60% of the top 1000 apps on the Play Store.

Kotlin for JavaScript (JS)

Kotlin/JS allows us to convert our Kotlin code, the Kotlin standard library, and suitable dependencies to JavaScript.

The kotlin.js and Kotlin. Multiplatform Gradle plugins are suggested for using Kotlin/JS. They offer a centralized and straightforward approach to setting up and managing Kotlin projects targeting JavaScript. This contains crucial features such as customizing our application's bundling, adding JavaScript dependencies straight from npm, and more.

Frameworks in Kotlin/JS

Frameworks that make it easier to construct web apps are extremely useful in modern web development. Here are some prominent web frameworks.

- **KVision:** KVision is an object-oriented web framework that allows us to construct Kotlin/JS apps with ready-to-use components that may be used as building blocks for our app's UI. We may develop our front end using reactive and imperative programming models, combine it with our server-side apps using connectors for Ktor, Spring Boot, and other frameworks, and exchange code with Kotlin Multiplatform.

- **fritz2:** fritz2 is a self-contained framework for creating reactive web UIs. It has its type-safe DSL for creating and generating HTML elements, and it uses Kotlin's coroutines and flows to define components and data bindings. It comes with state management, validation, routing, and other features, and it connects with Kotlin Multiplatform applications.

- **Doodle:** Doodle is a vector-based Kotlin/JS UI framework. Doodle apps generate UIs using the browser's graphics capabilities rather than DOM, CSS, or JavaScript. Doodle's technique allows us to precisely control the rendering of any UI components, vector shapes, gradients, and custom visualizations.

Kotlin/Native

Kotlin/Native is a technology that compiles Kotlin code to native binaries that can operate without using a virtual machine. It is a native implementation of the Kotlin standard library and an LLVM-based backend for the Kotlin compiler.

Why Is Kotlin/Native Used?

Kotlin/Native is primarily created to assist compilation for platforms where virtual machines are neither desired nor feasible, such as embedded devices or iOS. It is useful when a developer creates self-contained software that does not require a separate runtime or virtual machine.

Platforms of target Kotlin/Native is compatible with the following platforms:

- macOS

- Linux

- iOS, tvOS, watchOS

- Android NDK

- Windows (MinGW)

Kotlin for Data Science

Kotlin may be an excellent choice for working with data from establishing data pipelines to producing machine learning models:

- Kotlin is a compact, clear, and simple programming language.

- Static typing and null safety aid in creating dependable, maintainable code that is simple to troubleshoot.

- Kotlin, being a JVM language, provides excellent performance and the ability to leverage a whole ecosystem of tried-and-true Java libraries.

Editors Who Work Interactively

Notebooks like Jupyter Notebook and Apache Zeppelin are useful for data visualization and exploratory study. Kotlin interacts with these tools to assist us in exploring data, sharing our discoveries with others, and building up our data science and machine learning abilities.

- **Jupyter Kotlin kernel:** The Jupyter Notebook is a free and open-source web tool that lets us create and share documents, including code, visualizations, and markdown text. Kotlin-jupyter is an open-source project that adds support for Kotlin to Jupyter Notebook.

- **Zeppelin Kotlin interpreter:** Apache Zeppelin is a well-known web-based interactive data analytics application. It has extensive support for the Apache Spark cluster computing system, which is beneficial for data engineering. Apache Zeppelin includes a bundled Kotlin interpreter beginning with version 0.9.0.

Kotlin for Competitive Programming

Competitive programming is a mental sport where participants develop programs to solve precisely stated algorithmic challenges while adhering to severe limits. Problems can range from basic ones that can be solved by any software developer with minimal code to sophisticated ones that need an understanding of particular algorithms, data structures, and a lot of experience. While not explicitly designed for competitive programming, Kotlin fits well in this domain by reducing the amount of boilerplate that a programmer needs to write and read while working with the code almost to the level offered by dynamically typed scripting languages having the tooling and performance of a statically typed language.

Kotlin Language Applications

- Kotlin may use it to create Android applications.

- Kotlin may also compile to JavaScript, which the front end can then use.

- It is also intended for use in web development and server-side programming.

Setup of the Kotlin Environment for Command Line

We'll look at building up a Kotlin environment on a command-line compiler.

Installing Kotlin requires the following prerequisites: Because Kotlin runs on the JVM, we must install JDK and set the path in the local system environment variable.

Get the Kotlin compiler here: We can get the most recent version of the Kotlin standalone compiler from Github Releases. The most current version is 1.3.31.

Configure the Kotlin compiler for command-line use:

- First and foremost, extract the downloaded file to a location with write access.

- Copy the path up to the kotlinc bin directory.

- Now go to my computer's settings ->Advanced System Settings -> Environment Variables.

- Click the route in system variables and then click the edit button.

- Now, put the copied path to the bin directory into this field and click OK -> OK -> OK.

- In the command prompt, type kotlinc to confirm the installation.

Intellij IDEA Is Used to Build up a Kotlin Environment

JetBrains' Kotlin is a statically typed, general-purpose programming language that has been used to create world-class IDEs such as IntelliJ IDEA, PhpStorm, Appcode, and others. JetBrains initially offered it in 2011.

Kotlin is an object-oriented language superior to Java while remaining completely compatible with Java code.

Let's look at creating a Kotlin environment with Intellij IDEA and running our first Kotlin code:

- Install the most recent version of IntelliJ IDEA to get started. JetBrains' free Community Edition is available for download.

- Create a Kotlin application after installing Intellij IDEA. Creating a new project by selecting File -> New -> Project. Then choose Kotlin -> JVM | IDEA.

- Give our project a name and choose an SDK version. The project is called HelloEveryone in this case.

- HelloEveryone is our new project. Make a new Kotlin file in the source (src) folder and call it myfirstapp.kt.

- After we've created the file, write the main function. IntelliJ IDEA has a template for doing this quickly. Simply write main and press the tab key. Add a line of code that prints "Hello Everyone."

- Start the application.

- The program is now available to use. The simplest method is to pick Run "myfirstappKt" from the sidebar's green Run button. By hitting Ctrl + Shift + F10, we may run straight.

- The results will be displayed in the Run Tool Window if our program compiles appropriately.

Kotlin Hello Everyone Program

Hello, Everyone in any programming language is the first basic program. Let's start with writing the first program in the Kotlin programming language.

Kotlin's "Hello, Everyone" program: Open our favorite editor, notepad or notepad++, and create a file called myfirstapp.kt containing the code below.

```
// Kotlin Hello Everyone Program
fun main(args: Array<String>) {
    println("Hello, Everyone")
}
```

The program may be compiled using a command-line compiler:

```
$kotlinc myfirstapp.kt
```

Run the program now to view the output in the command-line compiler:

```
$kotlin myfirstapp.kt
```

Hello, Everyone

The following are the specifics of the "Hello, Everyone" program:

Line 1: The first line is a remark that the compiler ignores. Comments are made to programs to make the source code easier to understand for readers.

Kotlin accepts two types of comments:

- Single line comment:

  ```
  // This is a single line comment
  ```

- Multiple line comment:

  ```
  /*   This is
  multiple line
  comment
            */
  ```

Line 2: The main function is defined in the second line.

```
fun main(args: Array<String>) {
    // ...
}
```

Every program begins with the main() function. All functions in Kotlin begin with the fun keyword, followed by the function name (here main), a list of parameters, an optional return type, and the function body ({.......}).

In this scenario, the parameter – an array of strings and return units – is included in the main function. The unit type, which corresponds to void in Java, indicates that the function does not return any value.

Line 3: The third line is a statement that writes "Hello, Everyone" to the program's standard output.

```
println("Hello, Everyone")
```

Semicolons, like most current programming languages, are optional in Kotlin.

DATA TYPES IN KOTLIN

Primitive data types are the most fundamental data types in Kotlin, while all others, such as array and string, are reference types. To make basic data types act like objects in Java, wrappers (java.lang.Integer) are required, whereas Kotlin already contains all data types as objects.

In Kotlin, there are many kinds of data:

- Integer Data Type
- Floating-point Data Type
- Boolean Data Type
- Character Data Type .

Integer Data Type

Integer values are contained in these data types:

Data Type	Bits	Min Value	Max Value
Byte	8	−128	127
Short	16	−32768	32767
Int	32	−2147483648	2147483647
Long	64	−9223372036854775808	922337203685477580

Source Code:

```kotlin
fun main(args : Array<String>)
{
    var myint = 34
    //add suffix L for long integer

 var mylong = 22L
    println("My integer ${myint}")
    println("My long integer ${mylong}")
    var by1: Byte = Byte.MIN_VALUE
    var by2: Byte = Byte.MAX_VALUE
    println("The Smallest byte value: " +by1)
    println("The Largest byte value: " +by2)
```

```
    var St1: Short = Short.MIN_VALUE
    var St2: Short = Short.MAX_VALUE
    println("The Smallest short value: " +St1)
    println("The Largest short value: " +St2)

    var It1: Int = Int.MIN_VALUE
    var It2: Int = Int.MAX_VALUE
    println("The Smallest integer value: " +It1)
    println("The Largest integer value: " +It2)

    var Lt1: Long = Long.MIN_VALUE
    var Lt2: Long = Long.MAX_VALUE
    println("The Smallest long integer value: " +Lt1)
    println("The Largest long integer value: " +Lt2)
}
```

Floating-Point Data Type

Integer values are contained in these data types.

Data Type	Bits	Min Value	Max Value
Float	32	1.40129846432481707e-45	3.40282346638528860e+38
Double	64	4.94065645841246544e-324	1.79769313486231570e+308

Let's develop a program to represent the floating-point data type and its minimum and maximum values.

Source Code:

```
// Kotlin code
fun main(args : Array<String>) {
    var myfloat = 55F                       // add
suffix F for float
    println("My float value ${myfloat}")

    var Ft1: Float = Float.MIN_VALUE
    var Ft2: Float = Float.MAX_VALUE
    println("Smallest Float value: " +Ft1)
    println("Largest Float value: " + Ft2)

    var Dt1: Double = Double.MIN_VALUE
    var Dt2: Double = Double.MAX_VALUE
    println("Smallest Double value: " + Dt1)
    println("Largest Double value: " + Dt2)
```

Boolean Data Type

The Boolean data type simply represents one piece of information, either true or false. In Kotlin, the Boolean type is the same as in Java. The operations disjunction (||) and conjunction (&&) can be performed on Boolean types.

```
boolean       1 bit         true or false
```

Source Code:

```kotlin
// Kotlin code
fun main(args : Array<String>){
  if (true is Boolean){
       print("Yes,true is a boolean value")
    }
}
```

Character Data Type

Small letters (a–z), capital letters (A–Z), numerals (0–9), and other symbols are represented by the character data type.

```
char        8 bits        -128        127
```

Source Code:

```kotlin
// Kotlin code
fun main(args : Array<String>){
    var alphabet: Char = 'D'
    println("D is a character : ${alphabet is Char}")
}
```

VARIABLES IN KOTLIN

Every variable in Kotlin must define before it can utilize. An attempt to use a variable without declaring it results in a syntax error. The declaration of the variable type also determines the type of data that can store in the memory location.

The type of variable in the case of local variables may deduce from the initialized value.

```
var rollno = 54
var name = "Nidhi"
```

```
println(roll-no)
println(name)
```

Above is the local variable roll-no, whose value is 54 and whose type is Integer because the literal type is int, and another variable, name, whose type is String.

Variables in Kotlin are declared using one of two kinds:

- Immutable using val keyword

- Mutable using var keyword

Immutable Using val Keyword

Immutable variables are sometimes known as read-only variables. As a result, we cannot alter the variable's value specified using the val keyword.

```
val myName = "Gautam"
myName = "Preeniti"     // compile-time error
// It gives an error
```

Because it may be initialized with the value of a variable, an immutable variable is not a constant. It implies that the value of an immutable variable does not have to be known at compile-time, and if it is defined within a construct that is called repeatedly, it can take on a new value with each function call.

```
var myBirthDate = "01/11/1996"
val myNewBirthDate = myBirthDate
println(myNewBirthDate)
```

We can alter the value of a variable in a Mutable variable:

```
var myAge = 26
myAge = 27                 // compiles successfully
println("My new Age is ${myAge}")
```

Variable Scope

A variable exists just within the code block({............}) where it was defined. Outside of the loop, we cannot access the variable. The same variable can declare inside the nested loop – for example, if a function has an argument x and we create a new variable x inside the same loop, then the variable x inside the loop is different from the argument.

Naming Convention

LowerCamelCase should be used to name all variables.

```
val myBirthDate = "01/11/1996"
```

OPERATORS IN KOTLIN

Operators are special symbols that carry out various operations on operands. For example, + and – are addition and subtraction operators, respectively. Kotlin, like Java, has a variety of operators:

- Arithmetic operator

- Relation operator

- Assignment operator

- Unary operator

- Logical operator

- Bitwise operator

Arithmetic Operator

Operators	Meaning	Expression	Translate to
+	Addition	c + d	c.plus(d)
–	Subtraction	c – d	c.minus(d)
*	Multiplication	c * d	c.times(d)
/	Division	c / d	c.div(d)
%	Modulus	c % d	c.rem(d)

Source Code:

```
fun main(args: Array<String>)
{
   var c = 20 var d = 4 println("c + d = " + (c + d))
         println("c - d = " + (c - d))
         println("c * d = " + (c.times(d)))
         println("c / d = " + (c / d))
         println("c % d = " + (c.rem(d)))
}
```

Relation Operator

Operators	Meaning	Expression	Translate to
>	greater than	c > d	c.compareTo(d) > 0
<	less than	c < d	c.compareTo(d) < 0
>=	greater than or equal to	c >= d	c.compareTo(d) >= 0
<=	less than or equal to	c <= d	c.compareTo(d) <= 0
==	is equal to	c == d	c?.equals(d)? : (d === null)
!=	not equal to	c != d	!(c?.equals(d)? : (d === null)) > 0

Source Code:

```
fun main(args: Array<String>)
{
    var a = 20
    var b = 10
    println("a > b = "+(a>b))
    println("a < b = "+(a.compareTo(d) < 0))
    println("a >= b = "+(a>=b))
    println("a <= b = "+(a.compareTo(b) <= 0))
    println("a == b = "+(a==b))
    println("a != b = "+(!(a?.equals(b)?: (b ===
null)))))
}
```

Assignment Operator

Operators	Expression	Translate to
+=	c = c + d	c.plusAssign(d) > 0
-=	c = c - d	c.minusAssign(d) < 0
*=	c = c * d	c.timesAssign(d) >= 0
/=	c = c / d	c.divAssign(d) <= 0
%=	c = c % d	c.remAssign(d)

Source Code:

```
fun main(args : Array<String>){
  var c = 10
    var d = 5
    c+=d
    println(c)
    c-=d
    println(c)
```

```
    c*=d
    println(c)
    c/=d
    println(c)
    c%=d
    println(d)
}
```

Unary Operator

Operators	Expression	Translate to
++	++c or c++	c.inc()
—	–c or c–	c.dec()

Source Code:

```
fun main(args : Array<String>){
    var c=10
    var flag = true
    println("First print then increment: "+ c++)
    println("First increment then print: "+ ++c)
    println("First print then decrement: "+ c--)
    println("First decrement then print: "+ --c)
}
```

Logical Operator

Operators	Meaning	Expression
&&	return true if all expressions are true	(c>d) && (c>a)
||	return true if any expression is true	(c>d) || (c>a)
!	return complement of the expression	c.not()

Source Code:

```
fun main(args : Array<String>){
    var a = 110
    var b = 24
    var c = 11
    var result = false
    if(a > b && a > c)
     println(a)
    if(a < b || a > c)
     println(y)
```

```
        if ( result.not())
          println ("Logical operators")
}
```

Bitwise Operator

Operators	Meaning	Expression
Shl	signed shift left	c.shl(d)
Shr	signed shift right	c.shr(d)
Ushr	unsigned shift right	c.ushr()
And	bitwise and	c.and(d)
Or	bitwise or	c.or()
Xor	bitwise xor	c.xor()
Inv	bitwise inverse	c.inv()

Source Code:

```
fun main(args: Array<String>)
{
    println("4 signed shift left by 1 bit: " +
4.shl(1))
    println("11 signed shift right by 2 bits: : "
+ 11.shr(2))
    println("15 unsigned shift right by 2 bits:  "
+ 15.ushr(2))
    println("35 bitwise and 21: " + 35.and(21))
    println("35 bitwise or 21: " + 35.or(21))
    println("35 bitwise xor 21: " + 35.xor(21))
    println("13 bitwise inverse is: " + 13.inv())
}
```

KOTLIN STANDARD INPUT/OUTPUT

We will look at how to take input and show it on the screen in Kotlin. Kotlin standard I/O operations are used to transfer a series of bytes or byte streams from an input device, such as a keyboard, to the system's main memory and from the system's main memory to an output device, such as a monitor.

To print output on the screen in Java, we use System.out.println(message); however, in Kotlin, println(message) is used.

Kotlin Output – The fundamental action done to move byte streams from main memory to the output device is known as Kotlin standard output. We can output any of the data types integer, float, and any patterns or texts on the system's screen.

To display output on the screen, use any of the following functions:

```
print() function
println() function
```

Source Code:

```
fun main(args: Array<String>)
{
    print("Hello, Everyone ")
    println("This is tutorial of Kotlin.")
}
```

Distinction between println() and print()

The print() method outputs the message enclosed by double quotations.

The println() method outputs the message between the double quotes and advances to the start of the following line.

To print a string in Kotlin, use the following code:

```
fun main(args
          : Array<String>)
{
    println("Kotlin")
    println("A Computer Science portal for Geeks")

    print("Kotlin - ")
    print("A Computer Science portal for Kotlin")
}
```

Actually, print() calls System.out.print() and println() calls System.out. println().

If we're using Intellij IDEA, go to > Declaration by clicking the right button and then next to println. (In Windows, press Ctrl + B; in Mac, press Cmd + B.) It will open the Console.kt file, and we can see that it calls System.out.println inside().

Variables and Literals Print

```
fun sum(a: Int,b: Int) : Int{
    return a + b
}
fun main(args: Array<String>){
```

```
var a = 20
var b = 30
var c = 40L
var marks = 50.4
println("Sum of {$c} and {$d} is : ${sum(c,d)}")
println("Long value is: $e")
println("marks")
println("$marks")
}
```

Input of Kotlin

The core action done by Kotlin standard input is to flow byte streams from an input device, such as a keyboard, to the system's main memory.

We may obtain user input by using the following function:

```
readline() method
Scanner class
```

Take User Input with the readline() Function

```
fun main(args : Array<String>) {
    print("Enter the text: ")
    var input = readLine()
    print("We entered: $input")
}
```

Take Input from the User Using the Scanner Class

If we accept input from the user that is not of the String data type, we must use the Scanner class. To utilize Scanner, we must first import the Scanner on the top of the application.

```
import java.util.Scanner;
```

Create an instance for the scanner class and receive user input. In the following application, we will demonstrate how to accept integer, float, and Boolean data types input.

```
import java.util.Scanner
fun main(args: Array<String>)
{
    // create an object for scanner class
    val number1 = Scanner(System.'in')
```

```
    print("Enter integer: ")
    // nextInt() method is used to take
    // next integer value and store in enteredNumber1
variable
    var enteredNumber1:Int = number1.nextInt()
    println("We entered: $enteredNumber1")
    val number2 = Scanner(System.'in')
    print("Enter float value: ")
    // nextFloat() method is used to take next
    // Float value and store in enteredNumber2 variable
    var enteredNumber2:Float = number2.nextFloat()
    println("We entered: $enteredNumber2")
    val booleanValue = Scanner(System.'in')
    print("Enter boolean: ")
    // nextBoolean() method is used to take
    // next boolean value and store in enteredBoolean
variable
    var enteredBoolean:Boolean = booleanValue.
nextBoolean()
    println("We entered: $enteredBoolean")
}
```

Take User Input without Using the Scanner Class

We will use readline() to take user input and not import the Scanner class.

readline()!! To verify that the input value is not null, accept it as a string and follow it with (!!).

Source Code:

```
fun main(args: Array<String>) {
    print("Enter Integer value: ")
    val string1 = readLine()!!
    //.toInt() function converts the string into
Integer
    var integerValue: Int = string1.toInt()
    println("We entered: $integerValue")
    print("Enter double value: ")
    val string2= readLine()!!
    //.toDouble() function converts the string
into Double
    var doubleValue: Double = string2.toDouble()
    println("We entered: $doubleValue")
}
```

TYPE CONVERSION IN KOTLIN

Type conversion (also known as type casting) converts the entity of one data type variable into another data type variable.

As we all know, Java provides implicit type conversion from smaller to bigger data types. Long data type can be allocated an integer value.

As an example:

```
var myNumber = 110
var myLongNumber: Long = myNumber
```

However, implicit type conversion is not supported in Kotlin. An integer data type cannot be allocated an integer value.

```
var myNumber = 110
var myLongNumber: Long = myNumber          // Compiler
error
// Mismatch in type: the inferred type is Int,
although Long was anticipated.
```

In Kotlin, a helper function can be used to convert one data type to another explicitly.

Example:
```
var myNumber = 110
var myLongNumber: Long = myNumber.toLong()
```

To convert one data type to another, use the following helper function:

- toShort()
- toByte()
- toInt()
- toFLoat()
- toLong()
- toChar()
- toDouble()

It must notice that there is no help function for converting to Boolean type.

Conversion of a Larger Data Type to a Smaller Data Type

```
var myLongNumber = 12L
var myNumber2: Int = myLongNumber1.toInt()
```

Source Code:

```
fun main(args: Array<String>)
{

    println("258 to byte: " + (258.toByte()))
    println("40000 to short: " + (40000.
toShort()))
    println("21474847899 to Int: " + (21474847899.
toInt()))
    println("12L to Int: " + (12L.toInt()))
    println("21.54 to Int: " + (21.54.toInt()))
    println("21 to float: " + (21.toFloat()))
    println("55 to char: " + (55.toChar()))
    println("B to Int: " + ('B'.toInt()))
}
```

EXPRESSION, STATEMENT, AND BLOCK IN KOTLIN

Expression in Kotlin

An expression is made up of variables, operators, method calls, and other elements that all work together to generate a single value. Kotlin expressions, like any different language, are building blocks of any program that are generally constructed to produce new value. It can use to assign a value to a variable in a program at times. It should remember that one expression can include another.

- Variable declarations cannot be expressions (for example, var a = 110).

- A value assigned is not an expression (b = 14).

- A class declaration (class XYZ...) is not an expression.

Because every function in Kotlin returns a value of at least Unit, every function is an expression.

Source Code:

```kotlin
fun sumOf(a:Int,b:Int): Int{
    return a+b
}

fun main(args: Array<String>){
    val a = 12
    val b = 4
    var sum = sumOf(c,d)
    var mul = c * d
    println(sum)
    println(mul)
}
```

Both c * d and sumof(c, d) are expressions that return an integer value. sumOf() is a function that returns the sum of two arguments.

Kotlin if Expression

"If" is a statement in Java but an expression in Kotlin. It is referred to as an expression since it compares the values of c and d and returns the greatest value. As a result, is there no ternary operator (c>d)?c:d in Kotlin, because the if expression replaces.

if(condition) condition met, else condition doesn't meet.

Source Code:

```kotlin
fun main(args: Array<String>){
    val c = 1100
    val c = 989
    var e = 1022
    var max1 = if(c > d) c else d
    var max2 = if(e > c) e else c
    println("The maximum of ${c} and ${d} is $max1
" )
    println("The maximum of ${e} and ${c} is $max2
" )
}
```

Statement in Kotlin

A statement is a syntactic unit in any programming language that describes an action to be performed. A program is made up of a series of one or more statements. A statement in Java must always conclude with a semicolon (;), while in Kotlin, the semicolon (;) is optional.

- A variable declaration is a statement.

```
val marks = 99
var grade = 'A+'
```

- A statement is also created by assigning a value to a variable.

```
var sum = 11 + 21          // it is a statement
```

- In this case, 11 + 21 is an expression, but var sum = 11 + 21 is a statement.

Multiple Statements in Kotlin

When we write more than one statement in a single line, it is multiple statements.

Source Code:

```
fun main(args: Array<String>){
    val sum: Int
    sum = 110
    println(sum)                                // single
statement
    println("Hello");println("Everyone")        //
Mutilple statements
}
```

Block in Kotlin

A block is a section of software code enclosed by curly braces ({..}). A block can be made up of one or more statements, each preceded by variable declarations. A block contains one or more nested blocks. Every function has its own block, and the main function likewise has one.

```
fun main(args: Array<String>) {                 // main
block or outer block start
    val array = intArrayOf(3, 5, 7, 8)
    for (element in array) {                     // start
inner block
        println(element)
    }                                           // end inner block
}
```

Variable Scope in Nested Blocks

Unless a variable with the same name is declared at the head of the inner block, the variables declared at the block's head are visible throughout the block and any nested blocks. When a new declaration becomes effective throughout the inner block, the outer declaration reverts to being effective after the inner block. As a result, variables have nested scopes.

CONCLUSION

This chapter covered an overview of Kotlin, including how to set up a command-line environment and integrate it with Intellij. We also covered fundamental programming in Kotlin and data types, variables, and operators. In addition, we discussed Standard input-output in Kotlin. The last section discussed type conversion, expressions, statements, and blocks in Kotlin.

CHAPTER 2

Object-Oriented Programming (OOP) Concepts

IN THIS CHAPTER

➢ Class and object

➢ Constructor

➢ Inheritance

➢ Extension function

In Chapter 1, we discussed an overview of Kotlin, where we learned the introduction and its history and covered features and advantages. We also learned the environment setup for the command line and with IntelliJ. Moreover, we covered data types, variables, and input-output in Kotlin. In this chapter, we will discuss the Object-Oriented Programming's (OOP's) concept in Kotlin, where we cover class object, constructor, inheritance, and interfaces.

OBJECTS AND CLASSES IN KOTLIN

Kotlin supports both functional and OOP. In the previous section, we covered about functions, higher-order functions, and lambdas, representing Kotlin as an available language. This section will learn about the fundamental OOP's ideas that define Kotlin as an OOP language.

DOI: 10.1201/9781003311904-2

Language for Object-Oriented Programming

The fundamental ideas of an OOP language are class and object. These support OOP principles like inheritance, abstraction, and so forth.

Class

Class, like Java, is a blueprint for objects with comparable features. Before creating an object, we must first specify a class, and the class keyword is used to do so.

The class declaration comprises the class name, the class header, and the class body, all enclosed by curly braces.

Syntax:

```
class class-Name
{       // class header
   // property
   // member-function
}
```

- **Class name:** Each class has its name.

- **Class header:** Class headers are made up of a class's arguments and constructors.

- **Class body:** The class body is enclosed by curly brackets and comprises member functions and other properties.

The header and class body are optional; if there is nothing between the curly braces, the class body can be removed.

```
class emptyClass
```

If we wish to include a constructor, we must include the term constructor right after the class name.

Creating a constructor:

```
class class-Name constructor(parameters) {
   // property
   // member-function
}
```

Kotlin class example:

```
class employees
{
    // properties
```

```
    var name: String = ""
    var age: Int = 0
    var gender: Char = 'D'
    var salary: Double = 0.toDouble()
  //member functions
  fun names(){
    }
  fun ages() {
    }
  fun salary(){
    }
}
```

Object

It is an OOP core unit that represents real-world items with state and behavior. Objects are used to access a class's attributes and member functions. Multiple instances of the same class can create in Kotlin. An item is made up of:

- **State:** It is represented through an object's characteristics. It also reflects an object's attributes.

- **Behavior:** It is expressed through an object's methods. It also represents an object's interaction with other objects.

- **Identity:** It provides an object with a unique name and allows one thing to communicate with other objects.

Create an object: Using the class reference, we can create an object.

```
var obj = class-Name()
```

Accessing a class's properties: We may use an object to access a class's properties. First, use the class reference to build an object and then access the property.

```
obj.nameOfProperty
```

Accessing a class member function: We may use the object to access a class member function.

```
obj.funtionName(parameters)
```

Kotlin program for creating many objects and accessing the class's properties and member functions:

```kotlin
class employee
{// Constructor Declaration of Class
    var name: String = ""
    var age: Int = 0
    var gender: Char = 'F'
    var salary: Double = 0.toDouble()
    fun insertValues(n: String, a: Int, g: Char, s:
Double) {
        name = n
        age = a
        gender = g
        salary = s
        println("Name of the employee: $name")
        println("Age of the employee: $age")
        println("Gender: $gender")
        println("Salary of the employee: $salary")
    }
    fun insertName(n: String) {
        this.name = n
    }

}
fun main(args: Array<String>) {
    // creating multiple objects
    var obj = employee()
    // object 2 of class employee
    var obj2 = employee()

    //accessing the member function
    obj.insertValues("Praveen", 5, 'F', 50000.00)

    // accessing the member function
    obj2.insertName("Alie")

    // accessing the name property of class
    println("The Name of the new employee: ${obj2.
name}")

}
```

NESTED CLASS AND INNER CLASS IN KOTLIN

Nested Class

When a class is declared within another class, it is referred to as a nested class. Because nested classes are static by default, we may access their properties or variables using dot(.) notation without generating an instance of the class.

Syntax:

```
class outClass {
        . . . . . . . . . . .
        // properties of the outer class or a member
function
        class nestClass {
                . . . . . . . . . .
                // properties of the inner class or
member function
        }
}
```

Note that nested classes cannot access the members of the outer class, but we may access nested class properties from the outer class without generating an object for the nested class.

Program of accessing nested class attributes in Kotlin:

```
// outer class declaration
class outerClass {
    var str = "Outer class"
    // nested class declaration
    class nestedClass {
        val firstName  = "Pravi"
        val lastName = "Ruhi"
    }
}
fun main(args: Array<String>) {
    // accessing member of Nested class
    print(outerClass.nestedClass().firstName)
    print(" ")
    println(outerClass.nestedClass().lastName)
}
```

To access a nested class's member function in Kotlin, we must first build the nested class's object and then call the member function from it.

Program of accessing nested class member functions in Kotlin:

```
// outer class declaration
class outerClass {
    var str = "Outer class"
    // nested class declaration
    class nestedClass {
        var st1 = "Nested class"
        // nested class member function
        fun nestfunc(str2: String): String {
            var st2 = st1.plus(str2)
            return st2
        }
    }
}
fun main(args: Array<String>) {
    // the creating object of Nested class
    val nested = outerClass.nestedClass()
    //the  invoking the nested member function by
passing string
    var result = nested.nestfunc(" The member function
call successful")
    println(result)
}
```

In Comparison to Java

When it comes to features and use cases, Kotlin classes are quite close to Java classes but not identical. The Nested class in Kotlin is analogous to a static nested class in Java, whereas Inner class is comparable to a non-static nested class in the Java.

Kotlin	Java
Nested class	Static Nested class
Inner class	Non-Static class

Kotlin Inner Class

The term "inner class" refers to a class that can be declared within another class using the keyword inner. Using the inner class, we may access the outer class property from within the inner class.

```
class outerClass {
          . . . . . . . . . . . .
        // properties of the outer class or member
function

        inner class innerClass {
              . . . . . . . . . .
                // properties of the inner class or member
function
        }
}
```

In the following program, we attempt to access str from the inner class member function. However, it does not work and generates a compile-time error.

Inner-Class Kotlin Program

```
/ outer class declaration
class outerClass {
    var str = "Outer class"
    // innerClass declaration without using inner
keyword
    class innerClass {
        var st1 = "Inner class"
        fun nestfunc(): String {
            // it can not access the outer class
property str
            var st2 = str
            return st2
        }
    }
}
// main function
fun main(args: Array<String>) {
    // creating object for inner class
    val inner= outerClass().innerClass()
    // inner function call using object
    println(inner.nestfunc())
}
```

First, put the inner keyword before the inner class. Then, make an instance of the outer class; otherwise, we won't be able to utilize inner classes.

```
// outer class declaration
class outerClass {
    var str = "Outer class"
    // innerClass declaration with using inner keyword
    inner class innerClass {
        var st1 = "Inner class"
        fun nestfunc(): String {
            // can access the outer class property str
            var st2 = str
            return st2
        }
    }
}
// main function
fun main(args: Array<String>) {
    // for inner class creating object
    val inner= outerClass().innerClass()
    // using object inner function call
    println(inner.nestfunc()+" property accessed
successfully from the inner class ")
}
```

SETTERS AND GETTERS IN KOTLIN

Properties are an essential component of every programming language. In Kotlin, we may declare properties in the same way we declare variables. Properties in Kotlin can be specified as changeable using the var keyword or immutable using the var keyword.

Syntax:

```
var <propertyName>[: <PropertyType>]
[= <property_initializer>]
    [<getter>]
    [<setter>]
```

The property initializer, getter, and setter are all optional in this case. If the property type can infer from the initializer, we may also omit it.

The syntax of a read-only or immutable property declaration varies from that of a mutable property declaration in two ways:

- It begins with val rather than var.

- It does not permit a setter.

```
fun main(args : Array) {
    var x: Int = 0
    val y: Int = 1
    x = 2 // It can be allocated an unlimited
number of times
    y = 0 // It will never be allocated again
    }
```

In the above code, we attempt to assign a value to "y," but it generates a build time error since it cannot accept the modification.

Setters and Getters

The setter is used to set the value of a variable in Kotlin, while the getter is used to get the discount. Getters and Setters are produced automatically in the code. Let's define a "names" property in the "company" class. "names" has the data type String and will be initialized with a default value.

```
class company
{
var names: String = "Defaultvalue"
}
```

The preceding code is identical to the following code:

```
class company
{
    var names: String = "defaultvalue"
        get() = field                    // getter
        set(value) { field = value }     // setter
}
```

We create an object "c" of the class "company..". When we initialize the "name" property, we provide the setter's argument value, which sets the "field" to value. When we try to access the object's names property, we obtain a field because the code get() = field. Using the dot(.) syntax, we may acquire or set the properties of a class object.

```
val d = company()
d.names = "Hubtutor"          // access setter
println(d.names)              // access getter
```

Default Setter and Getter Kotlin Program

```
class company
{
    var name: String = ""
        get() = field          // getter
        set(value) {           // setter
            field = value
        }
}
fun main(args: Array<String>) {
    val d = Company()
    d.name = "Hubtutor"   // access setter
    println(d.names)                 // access getter
}
```

Identifiers for Values and Fields

In the preceding program, we have discovered these two identifiers:

- **Value:** Typically, we use the name of the setter parameter as the value, but we can use a different name if we want. The value parameter holds the value to which a property has been allocated. In the above program, we set the property name to d.name = "Hubtutor," and the value parameter holds the value "Hubtutor."

- **Backing Field (field):** It enables saving the property value in memory. When we initialize property with value, the value is written to the property's backing field. The value is allocated to the field in the preceding program, and subsequently, the field is assigned to get ().

Private Modifier

If we want the get method available to the public, we may use the following code:

```
var names: String = ""
    private set
```

Because of the private modifier near the set accessor, we can only set the name in a method within the class. A method within a class is used in a Kotlin application to set the value.

```kotlin
class company () {
    var names: String = "abc"
        private set

    fun myfunc(n: String) {
        names = n                    // we set the name here
    }
}

fun main(args: Array<String>) {
    var d = company()
    println("Name of the company is: ${d.names}")
    d.myfunc("Hubtutor")
    println("Name of the new company is: ${d.names}")
}
```

Explanation: We utilized the private modifier in conjunction with the set in this case. First, create an object of type company() and use $c.name to access the property name. Then, in the function specified within the class, we supply the name "Hubtutor" as a parameter. The name property is updated with the new name, and access is granted once more.

Setter and Getter with Custom Parameters

```kotlin
class registration( email: String, pwd: String, age:
Int,  gender: Char) {
    var email_id: String = email
        // Custom Getter
        get() {
            return field.toLowerCase()
        }
    var password: String = pwd
        // Custom Setter
        set(values){
            field = if(values.length > 7) value else
throw IllegalArgumentException("Password is small")
        }
```

```kotlin
        var age: Int = age
            // Custom Setter
            set(values) {
                field = if(values > 18 ) value else throw
IllegalArgumentException("Age must be 18+")
            }
        var gender : Char = gender
            // Custom Setter
            set (values){
                field = if(values == 'F') value else throw
IllegalArgumentException("User should be male")
            }
}

fun main(args: Array<String>) {

    val geek = registration("PRAViRUHi1998@GMAIL.
COM","Hub@123",25,'F')

    println("${hub.email_id}")
    geek.email_id = "HUBTUTOR@CAREERS.ORG"
    println("${hub.email_id}")
    println("${hub.password}")
    println("${hub.age}")
    println("${hub.gender}")

    // throw IllegalArgumentException("Passwords is
small")
    geek.password = "abc"
    // throw IllegalArgumentException("Age should be
18+")
    geek.age= 5
    // throw IllegalArgumentException("User should be
male")
    geek.gender = 'M'
}
```

CLASS PROPERTIES AND CUSTOM ACCESSORS IN KOTLIN

Encapsulation is the fundamental and most crucial concept of a class. It is a property that allows us to combine code and data into a single object. In Java, data is saved in fields, which are typically private. As a result, accessor methods – a getter and a setter – are supplied to allow the data to be accessed by the users of the specified class. Additional logic is implemented in the setter for delivering change notifications and verifying the passed value.

Property

In the case of Java, it is a mixture of accessories and fields. Properties are intended to be first-class language features in Kotlin. These features have taken the place of fields and accessor methods. A class property is declared in the same way as a variable, using the val and var keywords. A var-declared property is mutable and hence changeable.

Creating a class:

```
class Abcd(
    val names: String,
    val ispassed: Boolean
)
```

- **Readable Property:** Generates a field and a trivial getter

- **Writable Property:** A getter, a setter, and a field

Essentially, the property declaration declares the related accessors (both setter and getter for writable and getter for the readable property). The value is stored in a field.

Let's have a look at how the class is used:

```
class Abcd(
    val names: String,
    val ispassed: Boolean
)

fun main(args: Array<String>) {

    val abcd = Abcd("Bobi",true)
    println(abc.names)
    println(abc.ispassed)

    /*
    In Java
    Abcd abcd = new Abcd("Bobi",true);
```

```
System.out.println(person.getName());
System.out.println(person.isMarried());


*/
}
```

The constructor in Kotlin can be invoked without the need for a new key-word. Instead of using the getter, the property is directly addressed. The logic is same, but the code is significantly shorter. Setters of mutable properties operate identically.

Customer Accessors

Property accessor implementation on a custom basis:

```
class Rectanglee(val height: Int, val width: Int)
{
    val isSquare: Boolean
        get() {
            return height == width
        }
}

fun main(args: Array<String>) {

    val rectangle = Rectanglee(42, 44)
    println(rectangle.isSquare)
}
```

The property is Square does not require a field to contain the value. It just has a custom getter with the given implementation. The value is calculated each time the property is accessed.

KOTLIN CONSTRUCTOR

A constructor is a specific member function called when a class object is formed to initialize variables or attributes. A constructor is required for every class, and if we do not specify one, the compiler will build one for us.

There are two kinds of constructors in Kotlin:

- Primary Constructor
- Secondary Constructor

In Kotlin, a class can have one primary constructor and more subsidiary constructors. The primary constructor is responsible for initializing the class, whereas the secondary constructor is responsible for initializing the class and introducing some extra logic.

Primary Constructor

After the class name, the constructor keyword is used to initialize the primary constructor in the class header. The arguments in the main constructor are optional.

```
class Add constructor(val c: Int, val d: Int) {
    // code
}
```

The constructor keyword can be omitted if no annotations or access modifiers are supplied.

```
class Add(val c: Int, val d: Int) {
    // code
}
```

Program of primary constructor in Kotlin:

```
//main function
fun main(args: Array<String>)
{
    val add = Add(6, 8)
    println("The Sum of numbers 6 and 8 is: ${add.c}")
}
//primary constructor
class Add constructor(c: Int,d:Int)
{
    var a = c+d;
}
```

Explanation: When we build the class's object add, the numbers 6 and 8 are sent to the constructor. The constructor arguments *a* and *b* are initially set to 6 and 8, respectively.

The total of variables is stored in the local variable *a*. In the primary function, we use $add.a to access the constructor property.

Primary Constructor with Initializer Block

The primary constructor cannot include any code; however, the initialization code can insert in a separate initializer block preceded by the init keyword.

Kotlin primary constructor program with initializer block:

```
fun main(args: Array<String>) {
    val emp = employees(18118, "Sanik")
}
class employees(emp_id : Int,  emp_name: String) {
    val id: Int
    var names: String

    // initializer block
    init {
        id = emp_id
        names = emp_names

        println("Employees id is: $id")
        println("Employees name: $names")
    }
}
```

Explanation: When the object emp is formed for the class employee, the values 18118 and "Sanik" are supplied to the constructor's arguments emp id and emp names. The class id and names declare two attributes.

When an object is created, the initializer block is called, which initializes the attributes and prints to the standard output.

The default value in the primary constructor: We may initialize the constructor parameters with some default values, similar to initializing functions' default values.

In the main constructor of a Kotlin program, the following default values are used:

```
fun main(args: Array<String>) {
    val emp = employees(18118, "Sanik")
    // the default value for emp_name will be used
here
    val emp2 = employees(10011)
    //the default values for both parameters because
no arguments passed
```

```
        val emp3 = employees()
}
class employees(emp_id : Int = 110,   emp_name: String
= "abcd") {
        val id: Int
        var name: String

        // initializer block
        init {
            id = emp_id
            name = emp_name

            print("Employee id is: $id, ")
            println("Employee name: $name")
            println()
        }
}
```

Explanation: In this case, we've set the constructor arguments to the default values emp id = 110 and emp name = "abcd."

We gave the values for both arguments when we formed the object emp, which outputs those values.

However, the initializer block utilizes the default values and prints to standard output because we did not give the emp name when we created the object emp2.

Secondary Constructor

As previously stated, Kotlin may have one or more secondary constructors. Secondary constructors allow for variable initialization and the addition of logic to the class. The keyword constructor precedes them.

Program of Kotlin implementation of a secondary constructor:

```
//main function
fun main(args: Array<String>)
{
    Add(8, 6)
}
//class with one secondary constructor
class Add
{
    constructor(c: Int, d:Int)
```

```
    {
        var a = c + d
        println("The sum of numbers 8 and 6 is: ${a}")
    }
}
```

The compiler determines which secondary constructor will be invoked based on the parameters received. The above program does not indicate which constructor should be invoked, and the compiler makes the decision.

In a class, there are two secondary constructors in Kotlin:

```
fun main(args: Array<String>) {
    employee(18118, "Sanik")
    employee(10011,"Praveen",60000.5)
}
class employee {

    constructor (emp_id : Int, emp_name: String ) {
        var id: Int = emp_id
        var name: String = emp_name
        print("Employee id is: $id, ")
        println("Employee name: $name")
        println()
    }
    constructor (emp_id : Int, emp_name: String,
emp_salary : Double) {
        var id: Int = emp_id
        var name: String = emp_name
        var salary : Double = emp_salary
        print("Employee id is: $id, ")
        print("Employee name: $name, ")
        println("Employee name: $salary")
    }
}
```

In a class, there are three secondary constructors in Kotlin program:

```
//main function
fun main(args: Array<String>)
{
    Add(51, 61)
    Add(51, 61, 71)
```

```
    Add(51, 61, 71, 81)
}
//class with three secondary constructors
class Add
{
    constructor(c: Int, d: Int)
    {
        var a = c + d
        println("Sum of 51, 61 = ${a}")
    }
    constructor(c: Int, d: Int, a: Int)
    {
        var b = c + d + a
        println("Sum of 51, 61, 71 = ${b}")
    }
    constructor(c: Int, d: Int, a: Int, b: Int)
    {
        var e = c + d + a + b
        println("Sum of 51, 61, 71, 81 = ${e}")
    }
}
```

Using one secondary constructor to refer to another: Using this() method, a secondary constructor of the same class can invoke another secondary constructor. In the following program, we called another constructor (a,b,71) since it requires three parameters to be invoked.

Calling one constructor from another in Kotlin:

```
//main function
fun main(args: Array<String>)
{
    Add(51,61)
}
class Add {
    // calling another secondary using this
    constructor(c: Int,d:Int) : this(c,d,71) {
        var sumOfTwo = c + d
        println("The sum of two numbers 51 and 61 is:
$sumOfTwo")
    }
    // this executes first
```

```
    constructor(c: Int, d: Int,a: Int) {
        var sumOfThree = c + d + a
        println("The sum of three numbers 51,61 and 71
is: $sumOfThree")
    }
}
```

Calling the secondary constructor of the parent class from the secondary constructor of the child class: using the super keyword, we may call the parent class's secondary constructor from the child class's secondary constructor. We demonstrated the calling procedure below.

```
fun main(args: Array<String>) {
    Child(18118, "Sanik")
}
open class Parent {
    constructor (emp_id: Int, emp_name: String, emp_
salary: Double) {
        var id: Int = emp_id
        var name: String = emp_name
        var salary : Double = emp_salary
        println("Employee id is: $id")
        println("Employee name: $name")
        println("Employee salary: $salary")
        println()
    }
}
class Child : Parent {
    constructor (emp_id : Int, emp_name:
String):super(emp_id,emp_name,5000.55){
        var id: Int = emp_id
        var name: String = emp_name
        println("Employee id is: $id")
        println("Employee name: $name")
    }
}
```

KOTLIN VISIBILITY MODIFIERS

Visibility modifiers are used in Kotlin to limit the accessibility of classes, objects, interfaces, constructors, functions, properties, and their setters. There is no need to make getters visible because they have the same visibility as the property.

In Kotlin, there are four visibility modifiers:

Modifier	Description
Public	Visible everywhere
Private	Visible inside the same class only
Internal	Visible inside the same module
Protected	Visible inside the same class and its subclasses

If no modifier is supplied, it is public by default. Let's go through the modifiers above one by one.

Public Modifier

The default modifier in Kotlin is public. It is the most often used modifier in the language, and there are extra limits on who may view the part being modified. Unlike Java, there is no need to define anything as public in Kotlin – it is the default modifier if no other modifier is declared – public works the same in Kotlin as it does in Java. When the public modifier is applied to top-level items – classes, methods, or variables defined directly within a package – any other code can access them. If the public modifier is applied to a nested element – an inner class or function within a class – then any code that can access the container may also access this element.

```
// by default public
class C {
    var int = 20
}

// specified with public modifier
public class D {
    var int2 = 30
    fun display() {
    println("Accessible everywhere")
    }
}
```

Classes C and D are available from anywhere in the code, and the variables int and int2 and the method display() are accessible from everything that can access classes C and D.

Private Modifier

Private modifiers in Kotlin restrict access to code defined inside the same scope. It prevents access to the modifier variable or function from being available outside of the scope. Unlike Java, Kotlin enables several top-level declarations in the same file – a private top-level element in the same file can be accessible by everything else in the same file.

```kotlin
// class C is accessible from the same source file
private class C {
    private val int = 20
    fun display()
    {
        // we can access int in the same class
        println(int)
        println("Accessing int successful")
    }
}
fun main(args: Array<String>) {
    var c = C()
    c.display()
    // can not access 'int': it is private in class C
    println(c.int)
}
```

In this case, class C can only access from within the same source file, and the int variable can only be accessed from within class C. When we attempted to access int from outside the class, we met with a compile-time error.

Internal Modifier

The internal modifier is a newly introduced modifier in Kotlin that Java does not support. Internal signifies that it will only be available in the same module; attempting to access the declaration from another module will result in an error. A module is a collection of files that have been built together.

```kotlin
internal class C {
}
public class D {
    internal val int = 20
    internal fun display() {
    }
}
```

Class C is only available from inside the same module in this case. Even though class D may be accessed everywhere, the variable int and method display() are only available inside the same module.

Protected Modifier

The protected modifier in Kotlin only enables access to the declaring class and its subclasses. At the top level, the protected modifier cannot be disclosed. We used the derived class's getvalue() function to retrieve the int variable in the following example.

```
// base class
open class C {
    // protected variable
    protected val int = 20
}

// derived class
class D: C() {
    fun getvalue(): Int {
        // accessed from the subclass
        return int
    }
}

fun main(args: Array<String>) {
    var a = D()
    println("The value of integer is: "+a.getvalue())
}
```

Overriding of Protected Modifier

To override the protected variable or function in the derived class, we must mark it with an open keyword. In the following program, we override the int variable.

```
// base class
open class C {
    // protected variable
    open protected val int = 20


}
```

```kotlin
// derived class
class D: C() {
    override val int = 30
      fun getvalue():Int {
            // accessed from the subclass
          return int
      }
}

fun main(args: Array<String>) {
    var a = D()
    println("The overridden value of integer is: "+a.
getvalue())
}
```

Constructor Visibility

Constructors are always public by default, but modifiers may adjust their visibility.

```kotlin
class C (name : String) {
      // other code
}
```

We must express this explicitly by using the constructor keyword when modifying the visibility.

```kotlin
class C private constructor (name : String) {
      // other code
}
```

INHERITANCE IN KOTLIN

One of the most significant aspects of OOP is inheritance. Inheritance allows for code reuse by allowing all of the features of an existing class (base-class) to be inherited by a new class (derived-class). Furthermore, the derived class can add its features.

Syntax:

```kotlin
open class base-Class (x:Int ) {
    . . . . . . . . . .
}
```

```
class derived-Class(x:Int) : base-Class(x) {
    . . . . . . . . . .
}
```

By default, all classes in Kotlin are final. We must apply the open keyword in front of the base class to allow the derived class to inherit from it.

Kotlin inheriting properties and methods from the base class: We inherit all of its properties and functions when we inherit a class. We can utilize the variables and functions from the base class in the derived class and call functions from the derived class object.

```
//base class
open class base-Class{
    val name = "Hubtutor"
    fun C(){
        println("Base Class")
    }
}
//derived class
class derived-Class: base-Class() {
    fun D() {
        println(name)              //inherit name
property
        println("Derived class")
    }
}
fun main(args: Array<String>) {
    val derived = derived-Class()
    derived.C()           // inheriting the  base class
function
    derived.D()           // calling derived class
function
}
```

Explanation: There is a base class and a derived class in this case. When we instantiate the derived class, we generate an object, which is then utilized to call the base and derived class functions. The derived.C() function is used to invoke the C() function, which prints "Base Class." The derived.D() method is used to invoke the function D(), which prints the variable name inherited from the base class as well as the "Derived class."

Inheritance Use

Assume a corporation has three employees: a webDeveloper, an iOS-Developer, and an AndroidDeveloper. They all have certain characteristics in common, such as a name and an age and some unique abilities.

First, we divide the individuals into three classes, and each class has certain common and specific skills.

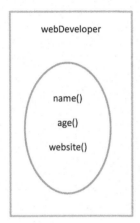
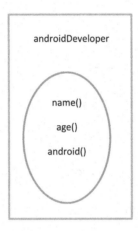
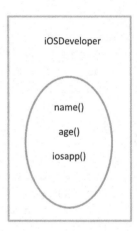

All three developers have the same name and age, but their programming skills are very different. We would be replicating the identical code for each character's name and age in each class.

If we wish to add a salary() function, we must duplicate the code in all three classes. This results in several duplicate copies of code in our program, which will almost certainly result in more complicated and chaotic code.

The work is made more accessible by employing inheritance. We may construct a new base class Employee that contains the features shared by the three original types. These three classes can then inherit common characteristics from the basic class and add their unique features. We can easily add the salary functionality to the Employee class without creating duplicates.

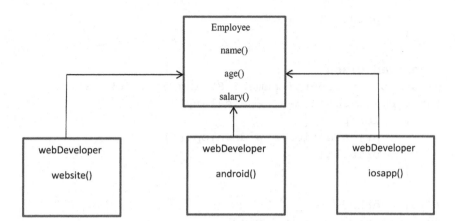

In this case, webDeveloper inherits all of the features from the base class and its feature website(). The same for the other two classes: iosDeveloper and androidDeveloper. It improves the readability and extensibility of our code.

Kotlin inheritance program:

```
//base-class
open class Employees( names: String,age: Int,salary :
Int) {
    init {
        println("Name is $names, $age years old and
earning $salary per month. ")
    }
}
//derived-class
class webDevelopers( names: String,age: Int,salary :
Int): Employees(names, age,salary) {
    fun website() {
        println("website-developer")
        println()
    }
}
//derived-class
class androidDeveloper( names: String,age: Int,salary
: Int): Employees(names, age,salary) {
    fun android() {
        println("android app developer")
```

```
        println()
    }
}
//derived class
class iosDevelopers( names: String,age: Int,salary :
Int): Employees(names, age,salary) {
    fun iosapp() {
        println("iOS app developer")
        println()
    }
}
//main method
fun main(args: Array<String>) {
    val wd = webDevelopers("Genna", 28, 12000)
    wd.website()
    val ad = androidDevelopers("Gautam", 29,14000)
    ad.android()
    val iosd = iosDevelopers("Praniti", 22,18000)
    iosd.iosapp()
}
```

Explanation: In this case, we have a base class Employees prefixed with the open keyword and includes the common characteristics of the derived classes. The Employee class has a primary constructor that takes three parameters: "name, age, and salary." There are three derived classes: webDevelopers, androidDevelopers, and iosDevelopers, all of which have primary constructors and three variables.

First, we create an object for the webDevelopers class and send the name, age, and salary to the derived class as arguments. It will set the values of the local variables and pass them to the base class. Then, using the object "wd," we execute the member function website(), which publishes the string to standard output.

Similarly, we make objects for the remaining two classes and call their member functions.

Primary Constructor for Kotlin Inheritance

If the derived class has the main constructor, we must initialize the base class constructor using the derived class's arguments. We have two parameters in the base class's primary constructor and three parameters in the derived class in the following program.

```
//base-class
open class Employees(names: String,age: Int) {
    init{
        println("The name of Employee is $name")
        println("The Age of an Employee is $age")
    }
}
// derived-class
class CEO( names: String, age: Int, salary: Double):
Employees(names,age) {
    init {
        println("The Salary per annum is $salary crore
rupees")
    }
}
fun main(args: Array<String>) {
    CEO("Suniti Pichai", 40, 420.00)
}
```

Explanation: In this case, we instantiate the derived class CEO and supply the parameters name, age, and salary. The derived class's local variables are initialized with the appropriate values, and the variable name and age are sent as arguments to the Employee class.

The employees class outputs the variable names and values to standard output before returning control to the derived class. The derived class then terminates after executing the println() command.

Secondary Constructor for Kotlin Inheritance

If the derived class lacks the main constructor, we must use the super keyword to call the base class's secondary constructor from the derived class's secondary constructor. We must additionally initialize the base class's secondary constructor using the derived class's arguments.

```
//base class
open class Employees {
    constructor(names: String,age: Int){
            println("The Name of Employee is $name")
            println("The Age of Employee is $age")
    }
}
```

```
// derived class
class CEO : Employees{
    constructor( names: String,age: Int, salary:
Double): super(names,age) {
        println("The Salary per annum is $salary
million dollars")
    }
}
fun main(args: Array<String>) {
    CEO("Sunidhi Nadela", 49, 220.00)
}
```

Explanation: We instantiate the class CEO and give the argument values to the secondary constructor in this case. It will initialize the local variables and use super to pass them to the base class Employees (name, age).

Overriding Member Functions and Properties

If member function with the same name exists in both the base and derived classes, we may use the override keyword to override the base member function in the derived class, but we must also mark the member function of the base class with the open keyword.

Program of overriding the member function in Kotlin:

```
// base class
open class Animals {
    open fun run() {
        println("The Animals can run")
    }
}
// derived class
class Tiger: Animals() {
    override fun run() {        // it overrides the run
method of base class
        println("The Tiger can run very fast")
    }
}
fun main(args: Array<String>) {
    val t = Tiger()
    t.run()
}
```

Similarly, we may override the base class's property in the derived class. **Program of overriding the member property in Kotlin:**

```kotlin
// base class
open class Animals {
    open var name: String = "Dog"
    open var speed = "50 km/hr"

}
// derived class
class Tiger: Animals() {
    override var name = "Tiger"
    override var speed = "120 km/hr"
}
fun main(args: Array<String>) {
    val d = Tiger()
    println(d.name+" can run at speed "+d.speed)
}
```

Calling the Superclass Implementation

We can call the base class member methods or attributes from the derived class using the super keyword. We call the base class's property color and method displayCompany() in the super class using the super keyword.

```kotlin
// base class
open class Phones() {
    var color = "White Gold"
    fun displayCompany(name:String) {
        println("The Company is: $name")
    }
}
// derived class
class iphone: Phones() {
    fun displayColor(){

        // calling the base class property color
        println("Color is: "+super.color)

        // calling the base class member function
        super.displayCompany("Apple")
    }
}
```

```
fun main(args: Array<String>) {
    val p = iphone()
    p.displayColor()
}
```

INTERFACES IN KOTLIN

Interfaces are Kotlin provided custom types that cannot be instantiated directly. Instead, these describe a type of behavior that the implementing types must follow. The interface allows us to create a collection of attributes and methods that concrete types must follow and implement.

Interfaces Creating

The interface declaration in Kotlin starts with the interface keyword, then the name of the interface, and finally the curly brackets that contain the interface's members. The distinction is that the members will not have their definition. The conforming types will offer these definitions.

Example:

```
interface Vehicles()
{
   fun start()
   fun stop()
}
```

Implementing interfaces: A class or an object can implement an interface. When we implement an interface, the conforming type must define all of its members. The name of the custom-type is followed by colon and the name of the interface to be implemented to implement an interface.

```
class Car: Vehicles
```

An example of an interface in Kotlin:

```
interface Vehicles {
    fun start()
    fun stop()
}

class Car : Vehicles {
    override fun start()
```

```
    {
        println("The Car is started")
    }

    override fun stop()
    {
        println("The Car is stopped")
    }
}

fun main()
{
    val obj = Car()
    obj.start()
    obj.stop()
}
```

Explanation: The interface vehicle specifies two methods in this application, start() and stop(), which must be overridden. Car implements the interface using class-literal syntax and overrides the two methods using the override keyword. Finally, the main function creates a Car object and calls the two functions.

Default Methods and Default Values
An interface's methods can have default values for its arguments. If a parameter's value is not provided at the function call time, the default value is utilized. Additionally, the methods may have default implementations. When the method is not overridden, they are used.
   Example of a default value and default method:

```
interface FirstInterface {
    fun add(c: Int, d: Int = 6)
    fun print()
    {
        println("This is a default method defined in
the interface")
    }
}
class InterfaceDemo : FirstInterface {
    override fun add(c: Int, d: Int)
```

```
    {
        val a = c + d
        println("Sum is $a")
    }

    override fun print()
    {
        super.print()
        println("It has been overridden")
    }
}

fun main()
{
    val obj = InterfaceDemo()
    println(obj.add(6))
    obj.print()
}
```

Explanation: The FirstInterface in the above program provides two methods: add() and print(). The add() function accepts two arguments, one of which has a default value of 6. A default implementation is also given for the print() function. So, when the class InterfaceDemo implements the interface, it uses the super keyword to override both methods and call the default implementation of print(). In addition, when using the add method in the primary function, only one parameter is needed because the second is set to a default value.

Interface Properties

Interfaces, like methods, can include attributes. However, because the interface doesn't have a state, they cannot be created, and hence there are no underlying fields to keep their values. As a result, the interface's fields are either left abstract or given an implementation.

Example of interface properties:

```
interface InterfaceProperties {
    val c : Int
    val d : String
        get() = "Helloo"
}
```

```
class PropertiesDemo : InterfaceProperties {
    override val c : Int = 6000
    override val d : String = "Property Overridden"
}

fun main()
{
    val x = PropertiesDemo()
    println(x.c)
    println(x.d)
}
```

Explanation: In the above program, InterfaceProperties specifies two properties: a, an integer, and b, which is of type String and has a getter. The class PropertiesDemo implements InterfaceProperties and adds value to the two properties. The method main generates a class object and uses dot-syntax to access its attributes.

Interface Inheritance

In Kotlin, interfaces can inherit from other interfaces. When one interface extends another, it can add its properties and methods, and the implementing type must define all of the properties and methods in both interfaces. An interface can inherit from many interfaces.

An example of interface inheritance:

```
interface Dimensions {
    val len : Double
    val br : Double
}

interface CalculateParameters : Dimensions {
    fun area()
    fun perimeter()
}

class XYZ : CalculateParameters {
    override val len : Double
        get() = 20.0
    override val br : Double
        get()= 17.0
```

```
    override fun area()
    {
        println("Area is ${len * br}")
    }

    override fun perimeter()
    {
        println("Perimeter is ${2*(len+br)}")
    }
}

fun main()
{
    val obj = XYZ()
    obj.area()
    obj.perimeter()
}
```

Explanation: The interface Dimensions in the program define two properties: len (length) and br (breadth). The CalculatedParameters interface inherits Dimensions and adds the methods area() and perimeter(). CalculatedParameters are implemented by the class XYZ, which overrides both the properties and methods, then executed in the main function.

Implementation of Multiple Interfaces

Because Kotlin classes follow the idea of single inheritance, each class can inherit just one class, interfaces support multiple inheritances known as multiple conformance in Kotlin. A class implements more than one interface as provided as it defines all of the interface's members.

Example of multiple interface implementation:

```
interface InterfaceProperties {
    val c : Int
    val d : String
        get() = "Helloo"
}

interface InterfaceMethods {
    fun description()
}
```

```
class MultipleInterface : InterfaceProperties,
InterfaceMethods {
    override val c : Int
        get() = 60

    override fun description()
    {
        println("The Multiple Interfaces implemented")
    }
}
fun main()
{
    val obj = MultipleInterface()
    obj.description()
}
```

Explanation: Two interfaces, InterfaceProperties and InterfaceMethods, are specified in the program. The class MultipleInterface implements these interfaces, and the methods are then executed in the main function.

DATA CLASSES IN KOTLIN

We frequently build classes to store data in them. Few standard functions are often derivable from the data in such classes. This class is known as a data class in Kotlin and is identified as such.

An example of data:

```
data class Students(val name: String, val roll_no:
Int)
```

The compiler generates the following functions automatically:

- toString()

- copy()

- hashCode()

- equals()

Data Class Creation Rules

To maintain consistency, data classes must meet the following requirements:

- At least one argument is required for the primary constructor.

- All primary constructor arguments must denote with val or var.

- Data classes are not allowed to be abstract, open, sealed, or inner.

- Data classes may implement only interfaces.

toString()

This function returns a string containing all of the data class's arguments.

First Example:

```
fun main(args: Array<String>)
{
    //declarion of a data class
    data class man(val roll: Int,val name:
String,val height:Int)

    //declarion of a variable of the above data
class
    //and initializing values to all parameters

    val man1=man(1,"man",40)

    //print all the details of the data class
    println(man1.toString());
}
```

For the automatically created functions, the compiler only uses the attributes defined inside the primary constructor.

It does not include the properties declared in the body of class.

Second Example:

```
fun main(args: Array<String>)
{
    //declarion of a data class
    data class man(val name: String)
```

```
    {
        //the property declared in class body
        var height: Int = 0;
    }

    //declarion of a variable of the above data
class and
    //initializing values to all parameters

    val man1=man("manisha")
    //class body properties must be assigned
uniquely
    man1.height = 80

    //this method print the details of class that
    //are declared in primary constructor
    println(man1.toString());

    //printing the height of man1
    println(man1.height);
}
```

copy()

Sometimes we need to replicate an object and update some of its attributes while keeping the others intact.

The copy() method is utilized in this scenario.

Copy() properties:

- It duplicates all of the parameters or members defined in the primary constructor.

- If declared, two objects might have the same main parameter values but distinct class body values.

copy() Declaration:

```
fun copy(name: String = this.a, age: Int = this.b) =
user(a, b)
```

where user is a data class: user(String, Int).

Example:

```
fun main(args: Array<String>)
{
    //declaring a data class
    data class man(val name: String, val age: Int)
    {
        //property declared in class body
        var height: Int = 0;
    }

    val man1 = man("manisha",19)

    //copying details of man1 with change in name
of man
    val man2 = man1.copy(name="rahi")

    //copying all details of man1 to man3
    val man3 = man1.copy();

    //declaring heights of individual men
    man1.height=110
    man2.height=92
    man3.height=130

    //man1 & man3 have different class body
values,
    //but same parameter values

    //printing info all 3 men
    println("${man1} has ${man1.height} cm
height")
    println("${man2} has ${man2.height} cm
height")
    println("${man3} has ${man3.height} cm
height")

}
```

hashCode() and equals()

- The hashCode() method returns the object's hash code value.

- The equals() function returns true if two objects have identical contents and operate similarly to "==", but differently for Float and Double values.

hashCode() Declaration:

```
open fun hashCode(): Int
```

hashCode() properties:

- Two hash codes specified twice on the same object will be equivalent.

- If two objects are equal according to the equals() function, the hash codes given will be the same.

```
fun main(args: Array<String>)
{
    //declaring a data class
    data class man(val name: String, val age: Int)

    val man1 = man("manish",19)
    val man2 = man1.copy(name="rahi")
    val man3 = man1.copy();

    val hash1=man1.hashCode();
    val hash2=man2.hashCode();
    val hash3=man3.hashCode();

    println(hash1)
    println(hash2)
    println(hash3)

    //checking equality of  these hash codes
    println("hash1 == hash 2 ${hash1.equals(hash2)}")
    println("hash2 == hash 3 ${hash2.equals(hash3)}")
    println("hash1 == hash 3 ${hash1.equals(hash3)}")

}
```

Explanation: Because man1 and man2 have the same object contents, they are equal and have the same hash code values.

KOTLIN SEALED CLASSES

Kotlin introduces a new type of class that is not seen in Java. These are referred to as sealed classes. As the name implies, sealed classes conform to constrained or bounded class hierarchies. Within a sealed class, a collection of subclasses is defined. It is used when it is known that a type will conform to one of the subclass types in advance. Sealed classes guarantee type safety by limiting the types that can match at compile time rather than runtime.

Declaration of sealed class: sealed class Demo

Simply use the sealed keyword before the class modifier to define a sealed class. Another distinguishing aspect of sealed classes is that their constructors are, by default, private.

Because a sealed class is implicitly abstract, it cannot be instantiated.

sealed class Demoo

```
fun main(args: Array)
{
    var d = Demoo()        //compiler error
}
```

Kotlin sealed class program:

```
sealed class Demo {
    class C : Demo() {
        fun display()
        {
            println("Subclass A of sealed class Demo")
        }
    }
    class D : Demo() {
        fun display()
        {
            println("Subclass B of sealed class
Demo")
        }
    }
}
fun main()
```

```
{
    val obj = Demo.D()
    obj.display()

    val obj1 = Demo.C()
    obj1.display()
}
```

It should be noted that all subclasses of the sealed class must specify in the same Kotlin file. However, they do not have to be specified within the sealed class; they can be defined where the sealed class is accessible.

Example:

```
//sealed class with single subclass defined inside
sealed class ABCD {
  class X: ABCD(){...}
}

// Another subclass of the sealed class defined
class Y: ABCD() {
    class Z: ABCD()    // This will cause an error.
Sealed class is not visible here
}
```

Sealed Class with When

Because the kinds to which a sealed class reference can conform are limited, it is most typically used with a when clause. This eliminates the need for the otherwise clause entirely.

Here's an example of a sealed class with a when clause:

```
// A sealed class with a string property
sealed class Fruits
    (val x: String)
{
    // Two subclasses of sealed class defined within
    class Apple : Fruits("Apple")
    class Mango : Fruits("Mango")
}

// A subclass defined outside the sealed class
class Pomegranate: Fruits("Pomegranate")

// A function to take in an object of type Fruit
```

```
// And to display an appropriate message depending on
the type of Fruit
fun display(fruit: Fruits){
    when(fruit)
    {
        is Fruits.Apple -> println("${fruit.x} is good
for iron")
        is Fruits.Mango -> println("${fruit.x} is
yummy")
        is Pomegranate -> println("${fruit.x} is good
for vitamin d")
    }
}
fun main()
{
    // Objects of different subclasses created
    val obj = Fruits.Apple()
    val obj1 = Fruits.Mango()
    val obj2 = Pomegranate()

    // Function called with different objects
    display(obj)
    display(obj1)
    display(obj2)
}
```

KOTLIN ABSTRACT CLASS

The abstract keyword is used in front of class to declare an abstract class in Kotlin. Because an abstract class cannot instantiate, we cannot create objects.

Declaration of an abstract class:

```
abstract class class-Name {
    .........
}
```

Remember the following:

- We are unable to generate an object for the abstract class.

- All variables (properties) and member functions of an abstract class are non-abstract by default. As a result, if we wish to override these members in the child class, we must use the open keyword.

- When we declare a member function as abstract, we don't need to annotate it with the open keyword because they are open by default.

- A derived class must implement an abstract member function since it doesn't have a body.

As demonstrated below, an abstract class can have both abstract and non-abstract members:

```
abstract class className(val c: String) {
// Non-Abstract Property
    abstract var d: Int        // Abstract Property

    abstract fun method1()    // Abstract Methods

    fun method2() {            // Non-Abstract Method
        println("Non abstract function")
    }
}
```

Program using both abstract and non-abstract members in an abstract class in Kotlin:

```
//abstract class
abstract class Employee(val name: String,val
experience: Int) {    // Non-Abstract

// Property
    // Abstract Property (Must be overridden by
Subclasses)
    abstract var salary: Double

    // Abstract Methods (Must be implemented by
Subclasses)
    abstract fun dateOfBirth(date:String)

    // Non-Abstract Method
    fun employeeDetails() {
        println("Name of the employee: $name")
        println("Experience in years: $experience")
        println("Annual Salary: $salary")
    }
}
```

```
// derived class
class Engineer(name: String,experience: Int) :
Employee(name,experience) {
    override var salary = 510000.00
    override fun dateOfBirth(date:String){
        println("Date of Birth is: $date")
    }
}
fun main(args: Array<String>) {
    val eng = Engineer("Praniti",3)
    eng.employeeDetails()
    eng.dateOfBirth("03 December 1996")
}
```

Explanation: The Engineer class in the preceding software is derived from the Employee class. For the Engineer class, object eng is created. While creating it, we gave two arguments to the primary constructor. This initializes the Employee class's non-abstract properties name and experience.

The eng object is then used to invoke the employeeDetails() function. It will print the employee's name, experience, and the override wage.

Finally, we use the eng object to call dateOfBirth() and provide the argument date to the primary constructor. It overrides the abstract fun of the Employee class and prints the value of to the standard output.

Using an abstract open member to replace a non-abstract open member: In Kotlin, we may use the override keyword followed by an abstract in the abstract class to override the non-abstract open member function of the open class. We shall accomplish that in the following program.

Program of overriding a non-abstract open function by an abstract class in Kotlin:

```
open class Livingthing {
    open fun breathe() {
        println("All living thing breathe")
    }
}
abstract class Animal : Livingthing() {
    override abstract fun breathe()
}
class Dog: Animal(){
    override fun breathe() {
```

```
        println("Dog also breathe")
    }
}
fun main(args: Array<String>){
    val lt = Livingthing()
    lt.breathe()
    val d = Dog()
    d.breathe()
}
```

Multiple Derived Classes

All derived classes can override an abstract member of an abstract class. We override the cal function in three derived classes of calculators in the program.

Program of overriding the abstract method in more than one derived class in Kotlin:

```
// abstract class
abstract class Calculators {
    abstract fun cal(a: Int, b: Int) : Int
}
// addition of two numbers
class Add : Calculators() {
    override fun cal(a: Int, b: Int): Int {
        return a + b
    }
}
// subtraction of two numbers
class Sub : Calculators() {
    override fun cal(a: Int, b: Int): Int {
        return a - b
    }
}
// multiplication of two numbers
class Mul : Calculators() {
    override fun cal(a: Int, b: Int): Int {
        return a * b
    }
}
fun main(args: Array<String>) {
    var add: Calculators = Add()
    var a1 = add.cal(5, 6)
```

```
println("Addition of two numbers $a1")
var sub: Calculator = Sub()
var a2 = sub.cal(11,6)
println("Subtraction of two numbers $a2")
var mul: Calculators = Mul()
var a3 = mul.cal(22,6)
println("Multiplication of two numbers $a3")
}
```

ENUM CLASSES IN KOTLIN

It is occasionally necessary for a type to contain just particular values in programming. The idea of enumeration was invented to do this. A named list of constants is an enumeration.

An enum has its specialized type in Kotlin, as it does in many other programming languages, signifying that something has several possible values. Kotlin enums are classes, as opposed to Java enums.

Some key facts to remember regarding enum classes in Kotlin:

- Enum constants are more than just collections of constants; they contain attributes, methods, and so forth.

- A comma denotes each enum constant function as a single class and instance.

- Enums enhance code readability by assigning predefined names to constants.

- Constructors cannot use to create an instance of the enum class.

Enums are defined by using the "enum" keyword in front of a class, as seen below:

```
enum class DAYS{
    MONDAY,
    TUESDAY,
    WEDNESDAY,
    THURSDAY,
    FRIDAY,
SATURDAY,
SUNDAY
}
```

Enums Initializing

Enums in Kotlin, like Java enums, can have a constructor. Because enum constants are Enum class objects, they may be initialized by supplying specific values to the primary constructor.

Here's an example of how to assign colors to cards:

```
enum class Cards(val colors: String) {
    Diamond("yellow"),
    Heart("white"),
}
```

We easily access the color of a card by using:

```
val colors = Cards.Diamond.colors
```

Enums Properties and Methods

Kotlin enum classes, like those in Java and other programming languages, include various built-in properties and functions that the programmer may utilize. Here are some of the most important approaches and properties.

Properties:

- **ordinal:** This property records the constant's ordinal value, typically a zero-based index.

- **name:** The name of the constant is stored in this attribute.

Methods:

- **values:** This function returns a list of all the enum class's constants.

- **valueOf():** This function returns the enum constant specified in enum that matches the input string. If the constant is missing from the enum, an IllegalArgumentException is produced.

To show the enum class in Kotlin, consider the following example:

```
enum class DAY {
    MONDAY,
    TUESDAY,
    WEDNESDAY,
    THURSDAY,
```

```
        FRIDAY,
        SATURDAY,
        SUNDAY
}
fun main()
{
    // A simple demonstration of properties and
methods
    for (day in DAY.values()) {
        println("${day.ordinal} = ${day.name}")
    }
    println("${DAY.valueOf(" FRIDAY ")}")
}
```

Properties and Functions of the Enum Class

The enum class in Kotlin provides a new type. This class type has its own set of attributes and methods. The properties can give a default value; however, each constant must declare its value for the property if no default value is provided. Functions are often defined within companion objects so that they do not rely on individual class instances. They can, however, be defined without the use of companion objects.

In Kotlin, an example is used to show properties and functions:

```
// Property with default value provided
enum class DAY(val isWeekend: Boolean = false){
    SUNDAY(true),
    MONDAY,
    TUESDAY,
    WEDNESDAY,
    THURSDAY,
    FRIDAY,
    // Default value overridden
    SATURDAY(true);

    companion object{
        fun today(obj: DAY): Boolean {
            return obj.name.compareTo("SATURDAY") == 0
|| obj.name.compareTo("SUNDAY") == 0
        }
    }
}
```

```
fun main(){
    // A simple demonstration of properties and
methods
    for(day in DAY.values()) {
        println("${day.ordinal} = ${day.name} and is
weekend ${day.isWeekend}")
    }
    val today = DAY.MONDAY;
    println("Is today a weekend ${DAY.today(today)}")
}
```

Enums as Anonymous Classes

Enum constants behave similarly to anonymous classes in that they implement their functions and override the class's abstract functions. The most crucial thing is that each enum constant is overridden.

```
// enum class defining
enum class Season(var weather: String) {
    Summer("hot") {
        // if not override the function foo() compile
time error
        override fun foo() {
            println("The Hot days of a year")
        }
    },
    Winter("cold") {
        override fun foo() {
            println("The Cold days of a year")
        }
    },
    Rainy("moderate") {
        override fun foo() {
            println("The Rainy days of a year")
        }
    };
    abstract fun foo()
}
// main function
fun main(args: Array<String>) {
    // calling foo() function override be Summer constant
    Season.Summer.foo()
}
```

Usage of When Expression with Enum Class

When enum classes in Kotlin are paired with the when expression, they have a significant benefit. The advantage is that because enum classes limit the values that a type may take when combined with the when expression and all of the constant definitions are supplied, the necessity for the otherwise clause is avoided. A compiler warning will be generated as a result.

```kotlin
enum class DAY{
    MONDAY,
    TUESDAY,
    WEDNESDAY,
    THURSDAY,
    FRIDAY,
    SATURDAY
    SUNDAY;
}

fun main(){
    when(DAY.SUNDAY){
        DAY.SUNDAY -> println("Today is Sunday")
        DAY.MONDAY -> println("Today is Monday")
        DAY.TUESDAY -> println("Today is Tuesday")
        DAY.WEDNESDAY -> println("Today is Wednesday")
        DAY.THURSDAY -> println("Today is Thursday")
        DAY.FRIDAY -> println("Today is Friday")
        DAY.SATURDAY -> println("Today is Saturday")
        // Adding an else clause will generate a
warning
    }
}
```

KOTLIN EXTENSION FUNCTION

Kotlin allows the programmer to extend the functionality of existing classes without inheriting them. This is accomplished through the use of a feature called extension. An extension function is a function that is added to an existing class.

To add an extension function to a class, create a new function that is attached to the classname, as demonstrated in the following example:

```kotlin
// A sample class to demonstrate extension functions
class Circle (val radius: Double){
```

```
    // member function of class
    fun area(): Double{
        return Math.PI * radius * radius;
    }
}
fun main(){
    // Extension function created for a class Circle
    fun Circle.perimeter(): Double{
        return 2*Math.PI*radius;
    }
    // create object for class Circle
    val newCircle = Circle(3.6);
    // invoke member function
    println("The Area of the circle is ${newCircle.
area()}")
    //invoke extension function
    println("The Perimeter of the circle is
${newCircle.perimeter()}")
}
```

Explanation: In this case, a new function is attached to the class using dot notation, with the function class Circle.perimeter() and a return type of Double. An object is created to instantiate the class Circle in the primary function, and the function is invoked using the println() statement. When the member function is called, it returns the area of the circle, whereas the extension function delivers the perimeter of the circle.

Extended Library Class Using an Extension Function

Not only may user-defined classes be expanded in Kotlin, but library classes can as well. The extension function may be added to library classes and used in the same manner that it can be introduced to user-defined classes.

The example below shows an extension function created for a user-defined class:

```
fun main(){

    // Extension function defined for Int type
    fun Int.abs() : Int{
        return if(this < 0) -this else this
    }
```

```
    println((-6).abs())
    println(6.abs())
}
```

Explanation: We used an extension function to expand the library function in this case. We used an integer value to do the modulus operation. We provided the integer values −6 and 6 and received positive results for both. If the parameter value is less than 0, it returns -(value), and if it is more than 0, it returns the same value.

Extensions Are Resolved Statically

The extension functions are resolved statically, which means that whatever extension function is executed relies entirely on the type of the expression on which it is called, rather than the type resolved on the final execution of the expression at runtime.

The following example will demonstrate the above point:

```
// Open class created to be inherited
open class C(val a:Int, val b:Int){
}
// Class D inherits C
class D():A(6, 6){}
fun main(){
    // Extension function operate defined for A
    fun C.operate():Int{
        return c+d
    }

    // Extension function operate defined for B
    fun D.operate():Int{
        return c*d;
    }

    // Function to display static dispatch
    fun display(c: C){
        print(c.operate())
    }

    // Calling display function
    display(D())
}
```

Explanation: If we're familiar with Java or another OOP language, we'll note that class D inherits class A. The parameter supplied to the show method is an instance of class D in the above program. According to the dynamic method dispatch paradigm, the output should be 36, but the extension functions are statically resolved, the operate function is called on type C. As a result, the output is 12.

Nullable Receiver

Extension functions can also be defined using the nullable class type. When the check for null is added inside the extension function, the proper value is returned.

A nullable receiver is an example of an extension function:

```
// A sample class to display name name
class ABC(val name: String){
    override fun toString(): String {
        return "Name is $name"
    }
}

fun main(){
    // An extension function as a nullable receiver
    fun ABC?.output(){
        if(this == null){
            println("Null")
        }else{
            println(this.toString())
        }
    }
    val x = ABC("Charch")
    // Extension function called using an instance
    x.output()
    // Extension function called on null
    null.output()
}
```

Companion Object Extensions

If a class has a companion object, we may also provide extension methods and attributes for the companion object.

Declaration of companion object:

```
class myClass {
    // the companion object declaration
    companion object {
        fun display(){
            println("The Function declared in
companion object")
        }
    }
}
fun main(args: Array<String>) {
    // invoking member function
    val ob = myClass.display()
}
```

Like regular member functions of the companion object, extension functions can call with merely the class name as the qualifier.

Example of a companion object extension:

```
class myClass {
    companion object {
        //the member function of companion object
        fun display(str :String) : String{
            return str
        }
    }
}

    // the extension function of companion object
fun myClass.Companion.abc(){
    println("The Extension function of companion
object")
}
fun main(args: Array<String>) {
    val ob = myClass.display("The Function declared in
companion object")
    println(ob)
    // invoking the extension function
    val ob2 = myClass.abc()
}
```

KOTLIN GENERICS

Generics are useful features that enable us to build classes, methods, and properties that are accessible using various data types while maintaining compile-time type safety.

Creating parameterized classes: A generic type is a type-parameterized class or function. We always use angle brackets () to define the type parameter in the program.

The following is the definition of the generic class:

```
class myClass<D>(text: D) {
    var name = text
}
```

To build an instance of such a class, we must provide the following type arguments:

```
val my : myClass<String> = Myclass<String>
("Hubtutors")
```

If the parameters can deduce from the constructor arguments, the type arguments can be omitted:

```
val my = myClass("Hubtutors ")
```

Because Hubtutors has the type String, the compiler figures out that we are discussing myclass<String>.

Advantages of generic:

- **Avoiding typecasting:** There is no need to typecast the object.

- **Type safety:** Generic permits just a single type of object at a time.

- **Compile-time safety:** Generics code is tested for parameterized types at compile time to avoid run time errors.

Generic Usage in Our Program

In the following example, we define a Company class with a single argument and a primary constructor. Now, we try to pass other data types in the Company class object, such as String and Integer. The primary constructor of the Company class accepts string types ("Hubtutors") but gives a compile-time error when an Integer type is passed (15).

```
class Company (text: String) {
    var y = text
    init{
        println(y)
    }
}
fun main(args: Array<String>){
    var name: Company = Company("Hubtutors")
    var rank: Company = Company(15)// compile time
error
}
```

To address the above issue, we may develop a user-defined generic type class that takes many parameters in a single class. The Company type class is a general type class that accepts both Int and String types parameters.

A Kotlin program using generic class:

```
class Company<D> (text : D){
    var y = text
    init{
        println(y)
    }
}
fun main(args: Array<String>){
    var name: Company<String> = Company<String>("Geeks
forGeeks")
    var rank: Company<Int> = Company<Int>(16)
}
```

VARIANCE

In contrast to Java, Kotlin makes arrays invariant by default. Generic types, by extension, are invariant in Kotlin. The out and in keywords might help with this. Invariance is the feature that prevents a standard generic function/class that has already been created for a specific data type from accepting or returning another data type. All additional data types are supertypes of Any.

There are two kinds of variation:

- Declaration-site variance (using in and out)

- **Use-site variance:** Type projection

The out Keyword

We may utilize the out keyword on the generic type in Kotlin to assign this reference to any of its supertypes. The out value can only be created by the specified class and cannot be consumed:

```
class OutClass<out D>(val value: D) {
    fun get(): D {
        return value
    }
}
```

We defined an OutClass class above that can return a value of type T. Then, for the reference that is a supertype of it, we may allocate an instance of the OutClass:

```
val out = OutClass("string")
val ref: OutClass<Any> = out
```

Note: If we did not utilize the out type in the preceding class, the next statement will result in a compiler error.

The in Keyword

We may utilize the in keyword on the generic type to assign it to the reference of its subtype. The in keyword may only use on parameter type that are consumed, not produced:

```
class InClass<in D> {
    fun toString(value: D): String {
        return value.toString()
    }
}
```

In this case, we've declared a toString() method that exclusively accepts D values. Then we may allocate a reference of type Number to its subtype – Int:

```
val inClassObject: InClass<Number> = InClass()
val ref<Int> = inClassObject
```

Note: If we did not utilize the in type in the preceding class, the following sentence would result in a compiler error.

COVARIANCE

Covariance states that substituting subtypes is permissible but not supertypes, i.e., the generic function/class may accept subtypes of the data type for which it is already defined, for example, a generic class created for Number can accept Int, while a generic class defined for Int cannot accept Number. This may be implemented in Kotlin by using the out keyword as seen below:

```
fun main(args: Array<String>) {
    val a: MyClass<Any> = MyClass<Int>()
// Error: Type mismatch
    val b: MyClass<out Any> = MyClass<String>()
// Works since String is a subtype of Any
    val c: MyClass<out String> = MyClass<Any>()
// Error since Any is a supertype of String
}
class MyClass<D>
```

We may immediately allow covariance by appending the out keyword to the declaration site. The following code works perfectly.

```
fun main(args: Array<String>) {
        val b: MyClass<Any> = MyClass<String>()
// Compiles without error
}
class MyClass<out D>
```

CONTRACOVARIANCE

It is used to replace a supertype value in the subtypes, i.e., the generic function or class may accept supertypes of the data type it is already defined. For example, a generic class defined for Number cannot take Int, while a generic class defined for Int may accept Number. In Kotlin, it is accomplished using the in keyword as follows:

```
fun main(args: Array<String>) {
        var x: Container<Dog> = Container<Animal>()
//compiles without error
        var y: Container<Animal> = Container<Dog>()
//gives compilation error
}
open class Animal
class Dog : Animal()
class Container<in D>
```

TYPE PROJECTIONS

It is feasible to copy all the members of an array of some type into an array of Any type, but for the compiler to compile our code, we must annotate the input argument with the out keyword. As a result, the compiler concludes that the input argument can be a subtype of the Any type.

Kotlin program for copying array elements into another:

```
fun copy(from: Array<out Any>, to: Array<Any>) {
    assert(from.size == to.size)
    // copying (from) array to (to) array
    for (c in from.indices)
        to[c] = from[c]
    // printing elements of array in which copied
    for (c in to.indices) {
    println(to[c])
    }
}
fun main(args :Array<String>) {
    val ints: Array<Int> = arrayOf(1, 2, 3,4)
    val any :Array<Any> = Array<Any>(4) { "" }
    copy(ints, any)

}
```

STAR PROJECTIONS

When we don't know what sort of value we're looking for and merely want to print all the items of an array, we use the star(*) projection.

Program of using star projections in Kotlin:

```
// star projection in array
fun printArray(array: Array<*>) {
    array.forEach { print(it) }
}
fun main(args :Array<String>) {
    val name  = arrayOf("Good","for","Good")
    printArray(name)
}
```

CONCLUSION

This chapter covered OOP's concept, where we learned class and object, nested class, constructors, and inheritances. We also covered interfaces, abstract class, and Generic Type in Kotlin.

CHAPTER 3

Exceptional Handling, Null Safety, and Regex and Ranges

IN THIS CHAPTER

➢ Exception handling | try, catch, throw, and finally

➢ Nested try block and multiple catch block

➢ Null safety

➢ Regex and ranges

In Chapter 2, we learned all the OOP's concepts in Kotlin, and in this chapter, we will cover exceptional handling where we cover try, catch, finally, and nested and multiple catch block in Kotlin. We will also cover null safety, including Type checking and smart casting. Moreover, we will learn Regex and Ranges in Kotlin.

EXCEPTIONAL HANDLING IN KOTLIN | TRY, CATCH, THROW, AND FINALLY

An exception is an unwelcome or unexpected occurrence during program execution, i.e., during run time, disrupting the usual flow of the program's instructions. Exception handling is a strategy for handling mistakes and preventing run-time crashes that might cause our application to crash.

Exceptions are classified into two types:

- **Checked Exception:** Exceptions are often put on methods and checked at build time, such as IOException, FileNotFoundException, etc.

- **Unchecked Exception:** Exceptions are often caused by logical mistakes and are checked at run time, such as NullPointerException, ArrayIndexOutOfBoundException, etc.

Exceptions in Kotlin

Exceptions in Kotlin are only unchecked and may be detected only at run time. All exception classes are descended from the Throwable class.

To throw an exception object, we often use the throw-expression:

```
throw Exception("Throwme")
```

Among the most common exceptions are:

- **NullPointerException:** When we try to execute a property or method on a null object, we get a NullPointerException.

- **Arithmetic Exception:** This exception is thrown when numbers are subjected to improper arithmetic operations. For example, divide by zero.

- **SecurityException:** This exception is thrown to signify a security breach.

- **ArrayIndexOutOfBoundsException:** This exception is thrown when we attempt to retrieve an array's incorrect index value.

Throwing an arithmetic exception in Kotlin program:

```
fun main(args : Array<String>) {
    var num = 20 / 0      // throws exception
    println(num)
}
```

In the above program, we start the num variable with the value 20/0, although we know that dividing by zero is not permitted in arithmetic. When we try to run the application, an exception is thrown.

To address this issue, we must employ the try-catch block.

Exception handling in Kotlin: In the following example, we divide an integer by 0 (zero), resulting in an ArithmeticException. The catch block will be executed because this code is in the try block.

In this scenario, the ArithmeticException happened; therefore, the ArithmeticException catch block run, and "Arithmetic Exception" was written in the output.

When an exception occurs, everything following that point is ignored, and the control immediately moves to the catch block if one exists. Whether or not an exception occurs, the finally block is always executed.

```kotlin
fun main(args: Array<String>) {
    try {

        var num = 30/0
        println("Beginners ")
        println(num)


    } catch (c: ArithmeticException) {
        println("Arithmetic Exception")
    } catch (c: Exception) {
        println(c)
    } finally {
        println("in any case it will print.")
    }
}
```

What If We Don't Handle Exceptions?

Assume that the program will end suddenly if we do not handle the exception in the preceding example.

Because we did not handle exceptions, the application ended with an error in this case.

How to Throw an Exception in Kotlin

The throw keyword may also use to throw an exception. The throw keyword is used to throw an exception in the following example. The statement preceding the exception was executed, but the statement after the exception did not perform because control was moved to the catch block.

```kotlin
fun main(args: Array<String>) {
    try{
        println("Before exception")
        throw Exception("Something went wrong ")
```

```
            println("After exception")
        }
    catch(c: Exception){
        println(c)

    }
    finally{
        println("can't ignore ")
    }
}
```

NullPointerException Example: Here's an example of a Null-PointerException thrown when a null String object's length() function is called:

```
public class ExceptionExample {
    private static void printLength(String str) {
        System.out.println(str.length());
    }

    public static void main(String args[]) {
        String myString = null;
        printLength(myString);
    }
}
```

In this example, the printLength() function uses the length() method of a String without first performing a null check. Because the string given from the main() function has no value, running the preceding code results in a NullPointerException:

```
Exception in thread "main" java.lang.
NullPointerException
    at ExceptionExample.printLength(ExceptionExample.
java:3)
    at ExceptionExample.main(ExceptionExample.java:8)
```

How to Avoid NullPointerException

The NullPointerException may avoid by employing the following checks and protective methods:

- Adding a null check before referring to an object's methods or properties to ensure that it is correctly initialized.

- Using Apache Commons StringUtils for String operations, such as StringUtils.isNotEmpty(), to check whether a string is empty before using it.

- Whenever feasible, use primitives rather than objects since they cannot have null references, such as int instead of Integer and boolean instead of Boolean.

KOTLIN TRY-CATCH BLOCK

In Kotlin, we utilize the try-catch block to handle exceptions in the application. The try block encloses the code responsible for throwing an exception, while the catch block handles the exception. This block must include in the main or other methods. Following the try block, there should be a catch block, a finally block, or both.

Syntax:

```
try {
    // the code that can throw exception
} catch(c: ExceptionName) {
    // catch exception and handle it
}
```

Kotlin application for handling arithmetic exceptions with a try-catch block program:

```
import kotlin.ArithmeticException

fun main(args : Array<String>){
    try{
        var num = 20 / 0
    }
    catch(e: ArithmeticException){
        // caught and handles it
        println("not allowed divide by zero")
    }
}
```

Explanation: In the preceding program, we utilized a try-catch block. Because the division by 0 is not defined in arithmetic, the num variable, which might throw an exception, is enclosed behind the braces of the try block. The catch block will catch an exception and run the println() function.

Kotlin Try-Catch Block as an Expression

As we have already established, expressions always return a value. We may utilize the Kotlin try-catch block as an expression in our software. The expression's return value will be either the final expression of the try block or the last expression of the catch block. If there is an exception in the function, the catch block returns the value.

Using try-catch as an expression in a Kotlin program:

```kotlin
fun test(c: Int, d: Int) : Any {
    return try {
        c/d
        //println("The Result is: "+ c / d)
    }
    catch(e:Exception){
        println(e)
        "Divide by zero not allowed"
    }
}
// main function
fun main(args: Array<String>) {
    // invoke test function
    var results1 = test(20,2  ) //execute try block
    println(results1)
    var results = test(20,0 )   // execute catch block
    println(results)
}
```

We utilized try-catch as an expression in the preceding code. Declare a function test at the program's head and use a try-catch block to return a value. We called the test function from the main method and passed the argument values (20, 2). The try result (20/2 = 10) is returned by the test function after evaluating the arguments. However, in the next call, we passed (b = 0), and this time the exception is caught and returns the expression of the catch block.

Kotlin Finally Block

In Kotlin, whether or not the catch block handles an exception, the finally block is always executed. As a result, it is utilized to execute critical code statements.

We can combine the finally block with the try block and then omit the catch block.

Syntax:

```
try {
    //the code that can throw exception
} finally {
    // code of finally block
}
```

Kotlin program of using finally block with a try block:

```
fun main(args : Array<String>){
    try{
        var ar = arrayOf(11,22,33,44,55)
        var int = ar[6]
        println(int)
    }
    finally {
        println("This block will always executes")
    }
}
```

In the preceding program, we utilized the try with finally block instead of the catch block. In this case, the catch block does not handle the exception, but executes the finally block.

Finally block with try-catch block Syntax:

```
try {
    // the code that can throw exception
} catch(c: ExceptionName) {
    // catch the exception and handle it.
} finally {
    // code of finally block
}
```

Kotlin program of using a finally block with a try-catch block:

```
fun main (args: Array<String>){
    try {
        var int = 20 / 0
```

```
        println(int)
    } catch (c: ArithmeticException) {
        println(c)
    } finally {
        println("This block will always executes")
    }
}
```

Kotlin Throw Keyword

To throw an explicit exception in Kotlin, we utilize the throw keyword. It is also capable of throwing a custom exception.

throw keyword in Kotlin program:

```
fun main(args: Array<String>) {
    test("abcde")
    println("executes after validation")
}
fun test(password: String) {
    // it calculate length of entered password and
compare
    if (password.length < 6)
        throw ArithmeticException("Password is short")
    else
        println("Password strong ")
}
```

NESTED TRY BLOCK AND MULTIPLE CATCH BLOCK IN KOTLIN

Nested Try Block

This part will learn about nested try-catch blocks and numerous catch blocks. A nested try block is one in which one try catch block is implemented inside another try catch block.

When an exception occurs in the inner try catch block that the inner catch blocks are not handled, the outer try-catch blocks are examined for that exception.

Syntax:

```
// the outer try block
try
{
```

```
    //the inner try block
    try
    {
        //the code that can throw an exception
    }
    catch(c: SomeException)
    {
        //it catch the exception and handle it
    }
}
catch(c: SomeException)
{
// it catch the exception and handle it
}
```

Nested try block Kotlin program:

```kotlin
fun main(args: Array<String>) {
    val numbers = arrayOf(11,22,33,44)

    try {
        for (i in numbers.indices) {
            try {
                var n = (0..4).random()
                println(numbers[i+1]/n)

            } catch (c: ArithmeticException) {
                println(c)
            }
        }
    } catch (c: ArrayIndexOutOfBoundsException) {
        println(e)
    }
}
```

Keep in mind that this result is created for a random integer. Don't worry if we obtain a different result because our result will be determined by the random number generated at that moment.

Multiple Catch Block

A try block may include several catch blocks. When we are unsure what sort of exception may occur inside the try block, we may insert numerous catch blocks for the various exceptions and the parent exception class in the last catch block to handle all the remaining exceptions that are not defined by catch blocks in the program.

Syntax:

```
try {
    // the code may throw exception
} catch(c: ExceptionNameOne) {
    // catch the exception one and handle it
} catch(c: ExceptionNameTwo) {
    // it catch the exception two and handle it
}
```

Program of multiple catch blocks in Kotlin:

```
import java.util.Scanner
object Tests {
    @JvmStatic
    fun main(args: Array<String>) {
        val scn = Scanner(System.'in')
        try {
            val n = Integer.parseInt(scn.nextLine())
            if (512 % n == 0)
                println("$n is a factor of 512")
        } catch (c: ArithmeticException) {
            println(c)
        } catch (c: NumberFormatException) {
            println(c)
        }
    }
}
```

Expression in catch block use: When expression in catch block may be used to replace several catch blocks in Kotlin. We will demonstrate how to utilize when expression in the following section.

```
import java.lang.NumberFormatException
import java.util.Scanner
object Tests {
    @JvmStatic
```

```kotlin
fun main(args: Array<String>) {
    val scn = Scanner(System.'in')
    try {
        val n = Integer.parseInt(scn.nextLine())
        if (512 % n == 0)
            println("$n is a factor of 512")
    } catch (c: Exception ) {
      when(c){
          is ArithmeticException -> { println("The
Arithmetic Exception: Divide by zero") }
          is NumberFormatException -> {
println("The Number Format Exception ") }
        }
      }
    }
}
```

NULL SAFETY

The goal of Kotlin's type system is to remove the risk of null references in code since it is a billion-dollar error. The NullPointerExceptions are thrown by the program at runtime, resulting in the application or system failure.

If we've ever written code in Java or another language that contains the idea of a null reference, we've probably seen a NullPointerException. If Kotlin compiler finds a null reference without executing any other statements, it raises a NullPointerException.

The following are some of the probable sources of NullPointer Exceptions:

- NullPointerException() is thrown explicitly.

- The !! Operator is used.

- Some data inconsistency in terms of initialization, for example, an uninitialized this being supplied as an input.

- Java interoperations include attempting to access a member on a null reference and generics types with erroneous nullability.

Nullable and Non-Nullable Sorts in Kotlin

The Kotlin type system distinguishes between two types of references: those that can hold null (nullable references) and those that cannot hold null (non-nullable references) (non-null references).

A String variable cannot contain the value null. If we try to assign null value to the variable, it gives a compiler error.

```
var st1: String = "Hub"
st1 = null // compilation error
```

We declare a variable as nullable string, typed String?, to allow it to retain null:

```
var st2: String? = "Huboftutors"
st2 = null // ok
print(st2)
```

Now, if we want to get the length of the string st1, it assures that it will not throw an NPE; therefore, we can confidently say:

```
val l = st1.length
```

However, accessing the length of the string st2 is not safe, and the compiler gives an error:

```
val l = st2.length         // error: variable 'st2'
can be null
```

A non-nullable Kotlin program:

```
fun main(args: Array<String>){
    // the variable is declared as non nullable
    var st1 : String = "Hubs"

    //st1 = null  // gives compiler error

    print("length of the string st1 is: "+st1.length)
}
```

If we try to assign null value to a non-nullable variable in this case, we get a compiler time error. However, if we try to read the length of the string, we will get a NullPointerException.

Nullable type Kotlin program:

```
fun main(args: Array<String>) {
    // the variable is declared as nullable
    var st2: String? = "Huboftutors"
    st2 = null    // no compile error
    println(st2.length)  // compile error because
string can be null
}
```

We may easily set null to a nullable type variable in this case. To retrieve the length of the string, however, we should use the safe operator.

Checking for the Null in Conditions

The most popular technique to check for null references is to use an if-else statement. We may check explicitly if the variable is null and handle the two possibilities independently.

Program for checking null in conditions in Kotlin:

```
fun main(args: Array<String>) {
    // the variable is declared as nullable
    var st: String? = "Huboftutors"
    println(st)
    if (st != null) {
        println("String of length ${st.length}")
    } else {
        println("Null string")
    }
    // assign null
    st = null
    println(st)
    if (st != null) {
        println("String of length ${st.length}")
    } else {
        println("Null String")
    }
}
```

It is important to remember that we used an if-else block to check for nullability. If the string includes null, the if block is executed; otherwise, the else block is executed.

Safe Call Operator(?.)

Null comparisons are straightforward, but the amount of nested if-else expressions might be difficult. As a result, Kotlin features a Safe call operator,?, which eliminates this complexity by executing an action only when the specified reference has a non-null value. It enables us to use a null-check and a method call in the same expression.

The following expression:

```
firstname?.toUpperCase()
```

is equivalent to:

```
if(firstname != null)
    firstname.toUpperCase()
else
    null
```

Kotlin program that employs the safe operator:

```
fun main(args: Array<String>) {
    // variable declared as nullable
    var firstname: String? = "Preesha"
    var lastname: String? = null
    println(firstname?.toUpperCase())
    println(firstname?.length)
    println(lastname?.toUpperCase())
}
```

If value is not null, we may use the safe call operator with let(), also(), and run().

A let operator can use to execute an action only when a reference contains a non-nullable value. The lambda expression included within the let is only run if the variable firstName is not null.

```
val firstname: String? = null
firstname?.let { println(it.toUpperCase()) }
```

Because the variable firstname is null in this case, the lambda expression to convert the string to Upper Case letters is not executed.

Program of using let in Kotlin:

```
fun main(args: Array<String>) {
    // creation of a list contains names
```

```
    var stringlist: List<String?> = listOf("Hub","of",
null, "tutors")
    // creation of new list
    var newlist = listOf<String?>()
    for (item in stringlist) {
        // only for non-nullable values executes
        item?.let { newlist = newlist.plus(it) }
    }
    // to print elements stored in newlist
    for(items in newlist){
        println(items)
    }
}
```

also() method chain with let():

```
fun main(args: Array<String>) {
    // creation of a list contains names
    var stringlist: List<String?> = listOf("Hub","of",
null, "tutors")
    // creation of a new list
    var newlist = listOf<String?>()
    for (item in stringlist) {
        // only for non-nullable values executes
        item?.let { newlist = newlist.plus(it) }
        item?.also{it -> println(it)}
    }
}
```

run() Method

To perform an operation on a nullable reference, Kotlin provides the run() function. It appears to be quite similar to let(), but inside a function body, the run() method runs only when this reference is used instead of a function parameter:

```
fun main(args: Array<String>) {
    // creation of a list contains names
    var stringlist: List<String?> = listOf("Hub","of",
null, "tutors")
    // creation of a new list
    var newlist = listOf<String?>()
    for (item in stringlist) {
```

```
       // only for non-nullable values executes
       item?.run { newlist = newlist.plus(this) }
// this reference
       item?.also{it -> println(it)}
   }
}
```

Elvis Operator(?:)

When original variable is null, the Elvis operator returns a non-null value or a default value. In other words, if the left expression is not null, the elvis operator returns it; otherwise, the right expression is returned. If the left-hand side expression is discovered to be null, the right-hand side expression is evaluated.

The following expression:

```
val name = firstname?: "Unknown"
```

is equivalent to:

```
val name = if(firstname != null)
       firstname
    else
       "Unknown"
```

Moreover, on the right-side of the Elvis operator, we may utilize throw and return expressions, which is very useful in the functions. As a result, instead of returning default value on the right-side of the Elvis operator, we can throw an exception.

```
val name = firstname?: throw
IllegalArgumentException("Enter a valid name")
```

Program of using Elvis operator in Kotlin:

```
fun main(args: Array<String>) {
    var st : String?  = "Huboftutors"
    println(st?.length)
    st = null
    println(st?.length?: "-1")
}
```

Not-Null Assertion (!!) Operator

If the value is null, the not null assertion (!!) operator changes it to a non-null type and throws an exception.

If someone wants a NullPointerException, he can ask for it directly using this operator.

```
fun main(args: Array<String>) {
    var st : String?  = "Huboftutors"
    println(st!!.length)
    st = null
    st!!.length
}
```

TYPE CHECKING AND SMART CASTING IN KOTLIN

Type Checking

At runtime, we may use the is operator in Kotlin to determine the type of a variable. It is a method of separating the flow for various objects by validating the type of a variable at runtime.

Program of type checking in Kotlin with if-else blocks:

```
fun main(args: Array<String>) {
    var names = "Praniti"
    var ages = 26
    var salary = 5100.54
    val employeeDetails: List<Any> =
listOf(names,ages,salary)

    for(attribute in employeeDetails) {
        if (attribute is String) {
            println("The Name is: $attribute")
        } else if (attribute is Int) {
            println("The Age is: $attribute")
        } else if (attribute is Double) {
            println("The Salary is: $attribute")
        } else {
            println("Not an attribute")
        }
    }
}
```

Explanation: In this case, we initialize three variables: name, age, and salary, which are then passed into the list. Then, using the for loop, we walk the list, check the element's type with the is operator in each if-else block, and execute the appropriate print() command in each if-else block.

Using When Expression

When expressions may simply replace if-else blocks, we will learn when expression in the control flow chapter. We can refer to when expression in Kotlin for further information.

Kotlin type checking program that employs when:

```kotlin
fun main(args: Array<String>) {
    var names = "Pariniti"
    var ages = 25
    var salary = 5100.55
    var emp_id = 13245f
    val employeeDetails: List<Any> = listOf(names,
ages, salary, emp_id)

    for (attribute in employeeDetails) {
        when (attribute) {
            is String -> println("Name is: $attribute ")
            is Int -> println("Age is: $attribute")
            is Double -> println("Salary is:
$attribute")
            else -> println("Not an attribute")
        }
    }
}
```

Smart Casting

In Java and other programming languages, explicit type casting on the variable is required before accessing its properties, while Kotlin uses smart casting. When a variable is passed through a conditional operator, the Kotlin compiler automatically changes it to a specific class reference.

Let's look at a Java example. First, we use the instanceOf operator to determine the type of the variable, and then we cast it to the target type, as seen below:

```java
Object obj = "Huboftutors";
if(obj instanceof String) {
    // Explicit type casting
    String st = (String) obj;
    System.out.println("length of String "
+ st.length());
 }
```

Smart type casting is one of the most exciting capabilities offered in Kotlin. To verify the type of a variable, we use the is or ! is operator, and the compiler automatically casts the variable to the desired type, as seen below:

```kotlin
fun main(args: Array<String>) {
    val st1: String? = "Huboftutors"
    var st2: String? = null    // prints String is null
    if(st1 is String) {
        // No Explicit type Casting needed.
        println("The length of String ${st1.length}")
    }
    else {
        println("String is null")
    }
}
```

Use of !is Operator

Similarly, we may verify the variable with the !is operator.

```kotlin
fun main(args: Array<String>) {
    val st1: String? = "huboftutors"
    var st2: String? = null  // prints String is null
    if(st1 !is String) {
        println("The String is null")
    }
    else {
        println("The length of String ${st1.length}")
    }
}
```

Smart casts do not operate if the compiler cannot ensure that the variable will not change between the check and the usage. The following guidelines regulate the use of smart casts:

- Except for local delegated properties, val local variables always works.

- val properties only work if the property is private or internal, or if the check is done in the same module as the property is defined. Smart casts do not work on open properties or properties with custom getters.

- var local variables only work if the variable has not been modified between the check and usage, is not captured in lambda that modifies it, and is not a local delegated property.

- Because the variable can change at any time, var properties never operate.

EXPLICIT TYPE CASTING IN KOTLIN

To check the type of a variable in Smart Casting, we usually use the is or!is operator, and the compiler automatically casts the variable to the target type, while in explicit type casting, we use the as operator.

Explicit type casting can be accomplished by employing:

- Unsafe cast operator: as

- Safe cast operator: as?

Unsafe Cast Operator: as

We utilize the type cast operator to cast a variable to the target type manually.

Variable st1 of string type is cast to target type using as operator in the following program.

```
fun main(args: Array<String>) {
    val st1: String = "works fine"
    val st2: String = st1 as String        // Works
    println(st1)
}
```

It is possible that we cannot cast a variable to the target type, and it throws an exception at runtime, which is why it is called unsafe casting.

When an Integer type is used to cast to a String type, a ClassCastException is thrown.

```
fun main(args: Array<String>){
    val st1: Any = 13
    val st2: String = st1 as String        // throw
exception
    println(st1)
}
```

We cannot cast a nullable string to a non-nullabe string, and an exception is thrown as TypeCastException.

```
fun main(args: Array<String>){
    val st1: String? = null
    val st2: String = st1 as String        // throw
exception
    println(st1)
}
```

As a result, we must utilize the target type as a nullable String as well, so that type casting does not cause an exception.

```
fun main(args: Array<String>){
    val st1: String? = null
    val st2: String? = st1 as String?      // throw
exception
    println(st1)
}
```

Safe Cast Operator: as?

Kotlin also provides type casting using the safe cast operator, as? If casting is not possible, the method returns null value rather than throwing a ClassCastException error.

Here's an example: it works great if we try to cast any sort of string value that the programmer is familiar with into a nullable string. When we initialize the Any with an integer value and try to cast it into a nullable string, the type casting fails and returns null to st3.

```
fun main(args: Array<String>){
    var st1: Any = "Safe casting"
```

```
    val st2: String? = st1 as? String      // it works
    st1 = 13
    // the type casting not possible so returns null
to st3
    val st3: String? = st1 as? String
    val st4: Int? = st1 as? Int             // it works
    println(st2)
    println(st3)
    println(st4)
}
```

REGEX AND RANGES

Regular Expressions in Kotlin

Regular Expressions are a basic feature of almost every programming language, including Kotlin. The Regex class in Kotlin provides support for regular expressions. This class's objects represent regular expressions that may use for string matching.

```
class Regex
```

Regular expressions may be found in a wide range of software, from the most basic to the most complicated.

Constructors:

- **<init>(pattern: String):** This constructor creates a regular expression based on the pattern string.

- **(pattern: String, option: RegexOption):** This constructor generates a regular expression based on the pattern and option specified. The option is a constant of the RegexOption enum class.

- **(pattern: String, options: Set<RegexOption>):** This constructor creates a regular expression based on the specified string pattern and the set of options.

Properties:

- **val options: Set<RegexOption>:** It includes the set of options that must be utilized while creating a regex.

- **val pattern: String:** It holds the pattern's description string.

Regex Functions

containsMatchIn(): This function returns a boolean indicating whether our pattern is matched in the input.

```
fun containsMatchIn(input: CharSequence): Boolean
```

This example will show how to use the containsMatchIn() method in Kotlin:

```
fun main()
{
    // A regex to match any string starting with the
letter 'a'
    val pattern = Regex("^a")
    println(pattern.containsMatchIn("abcd"))
    println(pattern.containsMatchIn("bacd"))
}
```

find(): From the specified beginning index, this method returns the first matched substring pertaining to our pattern in the input.

```
fun find(input: CharSequence, start_Index: Int): MatchResult?
```

This example will show how to use the find() method in Kotlin:

```
fun main()
{
    // Regex to match "ll" in a string
    val pattern1 = Regex("ll")
    val ans : MatchResult? = pattern1.
find("HellooHelloo", 6)
    println(ans?.value)
}
```

findAll(): This method returns all matchings of the supplied pattern in the input, beginning with the start index specified.

```
fun findAll(
    input: CharSequence,
    start_Index: Int
): Sequence
```

This example will show how to use the findAll method in Kotlin:

```
fun main()
{
    // A Regex to match a 3 letter pattern beginning
with ab
    val pattern2 = Regex("ab.")
    val ans1 : Sequence<MatchResult> = pattern2.
findAll("absfffgdbabc", 0)
    // forEach loop used to display all matches
    ans1.forEach()
    {
            matchResult -> println(matchResult.value)
    }
    println()
}
```

matches(): This method returns a boolean indicating whether the input string matches the pattern entirely or not.

```
infix fun matches(input: Char_Sequence): Boolean
```

This example will show how to use the matches() method in Kotlin:

```
fun main()
{
    //to tests the demonstrating entire string match
    val pattern = Regex("h([ee]+)ks?")
    println(pattern.matches("heeks"))
    println(pattern.matches("heeeeeeeeeeks"))
    println(pattern.matches("heeksforheeks"))
}
```

matchEntire(): This method attempts to match the full input to the specified pattern string and returns the string if it does. Return a null if it does not match the string.

```
fun matchEntire(input: Char_Sequence): MatchResult?
```

This example will show how to use the matchEntire() method in Kotlin:

```
fun main()
{
    // Tests demonstrating entire string match
    var pattern = Regex("heeks?")
    println(pattern.matchEntire("heeks")?.value)
    println(pattern.matchEntire("heeeeeeeks")?.value)
    pattern = Regex("""\D+""")
    println(pattern.matchEntire("heeks")?.value)
    println(pattern.matchEntire("heeks13245")?.value)
}
```

replace(): This function replaces all pattern occurrences in the input string with the replacement string specified.

fun replace(input: Char_Sequence, replacement: String): String

replaceFirst(): This function replaces the replacement string with the first regular expression match in the input.

```
fun replaceFirst(
    input: Char_Sequence,
    replacement: String
): String
```

In Kotlin, here's an example of the replace() and replaceFirst() work methods:

```
fun main()
{
    // Tests demonstrating replacement functions
    val pattern4 = Regex("xyzz")
    // replace all xyzz with abcd in the string
    println(pattern4.replace("xyzzxyzzzzzzzzz",
"abcd"))
    // replace only first xyz with abc not all
    println(pattern4.replaceFirst("xyzzdddddddxyzz",
"abcd"))
    println()
}
```

split(): This function divides the input string into tokens based on the parameter value.

```
fun split(input: Char_Sequence, limit: Int): List
```

This example will show how to use the split() method in Kotlin:

```
fun main()
{
    // Tests demonstrating split function
    val pattern = Regex("\\s+")  // separate for
white-spaces
    val ans : List<String> = pattern.split("This is a
class")
    ans.forEach { word -> println(word) }
}
```

RANGES IN KOTLIN

The range in Kotlin is a set of finite values specified by endpoints. In Kotlin, a range consists of a start, a stop, and a step. The start and finish points in the Range are inclusive, and the step value is set to 1 by default.

The range is used with comparable kinds.

Range may create in three ways in Kotlin:

- Using (..) operator

- Using rangeTo() function

- Using downTo() function

(..) Operator

It is the most basic approach to interact with range. It will generate a range from start to finish that includes both the start and end values. It is the rangeTo() function's operator form. We may create ranges for integers and characters by using the (..) operator.

In Kotlin, use the (..) operator to create an integer range program:

```
fun main(args : Array<String>){
    println("Integer-range:")
    // creation of integer range
    for(num in 1..5){
```

```kotlin
        println(num)
    }
}
```

Character range Kotlin program using the (..) operator:

```kotlin
fun main(args : Array<String>){
    println("Character-range:")
    // creation of character range
    for(ch in 'a'..'e'){
        println(ch)
    }
}
```

rangeTo() Function

It is similar to the (..) operator. It will generate a range up to the value specified as an argument. It is also used to create range for numbers and characters.

Program of using the rangeTo() method in Kotlin to create an integer range:

```kotlin
fun main(args : Array<String>){
    println("Integer-range:")
    // creation of integer range
    for(num in 1.rangeTo(5)){
        println(num)
    }
}
```

of using the rangeTo() method in Kotlin to create a character range:

```kotlin
fun main(args : Array<String>){
    println("Character -range:")
    // creation of character range
    for(ch in 'a'.rangeTo('e')){
        println(ch)
    }
}
```

downTo() Function

It is the reverse of the rangeTo() or (..). It generates a range in decreasing order, from larger to smaller numbers. This section will define ranges in reverse order for both integers and characters.

Kotlin program with an integer range that uses the downTo() function:

```
fun main(args : Array<String>){
    println("The Integer range in descending order:")
    // creation of integer range
    for(nums in 5.downTo(1)){
        println(nums)
    }
}
```

Program of character range using downTo() function in Kotlin:

```
fun main(args : Array<String>){
    println("The Character range in reverse order:")
    // creation of character range
    for(ch in 'e'.downTo('a')){
        println(ch)
    }
}
```

Range Using forEach Loop

```
The forEach loop is also used to loop through the
range.
fun main(args : Array<String>){
    println("Integer-range:")
    // creation integer range
    (2..5).forEach(::println)
}
```

step(): The keyword step can use to create a step between values. It is mainly used to give the space between two values in rangeTo(), downTo(), or the (..) operator. The default value for step is 1; therefore, the step function cannot have a value of zero.

The following is a step-by-step Kotlin program:

```kotlin
fun main(args: Array<String>) {
    //for iterating over range
    var i = 2
    // for loop with the step keyword
    for (i in 3..10 step 2)
        print("$i ")
    println()
    // print the first value of the range
    println((11..20 step 2).first)
    // print last value of the range
    println((11..20 step 4).last)
    // print the the step used in the range
    println((11..20 step 5).step)
}
```

reversed function(): It's used to reverse the specified range type. We may use the reverse() method instead of downTo() to print the range in descending order.

```kotlin
fun main(args: Array<String>) {
    var range = 3..8
    for (y in range.reversed()){
        print("$y ")
    }
}
```

Various predefined functions in range: The following functions are predefined in Kotlin Range: min(), max(), sum(), and average ().

```kotlin
fun main() {
    val predefined = (15..20)
    println("minimum value of the range is:
"+predefined.min())
    println("maximum value of the range is:
"+predefined.max())
    println("sum of all values of the range is:
"+predefined.sum())
    println("average value of the range is:
"+predefined.average())
}
```

Check to see whether a value is inside a range:

```
fun main(args: Array<String>)
{
    var i = 3
    //to check whether value lies in the range
    if( i in 5..10)
        println("$i is lie within range")
    else
        println("$i does not lie within range")
}
```

CONCLUSION

In this chapter, we covered Exceptional handling with try, catch, throw, and finally, and we also covered try block and multiple catch blocks. Moreover, we learned about Null safety and Regex and Ranges in Kotlin.

CHAPTER 4

Control Flow Statements

IN THIS CHAPTER

> ➤ If-else

> ➤ While, do-while

> ➤ For loop

> ➤ Labeled and unlabeled break

> ➤ Labeled and unlabeled continue

Chapter 3 covered expression handling, null safety, and regex and ranges. In this chapter, we will cover the control flow statement in Kotlin.

IF-ELSE EXPRESSION IN KOTLIN

Making decisions in programming is similar to making decisions in real life. When a given condition is met in programming, a particular code block must be performed. Regulate statements are used in programming languages to control program execution flow based on specific conditions. If the condition is met, the program enters the conditional block and performs the instructions.

In Kotlin, there are several forms of if-else expressions:

- if expression

- if-else expression

DOI: 10.1201/9781003311904-4

- if-else-if ladder expression
- nested if expression

If Statement

It is used to describe whether a block of statements should be executed or not, i.e., if a given condition is true, then the statement or block of statements should execute; otherwise, the statement or block of statements should not run.

Syntax:

```
if(condition) {
        // the code to run if condition is true
}
```

Flowchart:

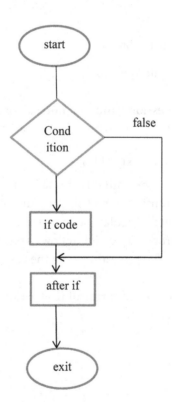

Statement of if.

Example:

```kotlin
fun main(args: Array<String>) {
    var c = 3
    if(c > 0){
        print("Yes,the number is positive")
    }
}
```

If-Else Statement

The if-else statement is made up of two blocks of statements. When the condition is true, the "if" statement is used to run the block of code, and when the condition is false, the "else" statement is used to execute the block of code.

Syntax:

```
if(condition) {
        // the code to run if condition is true
}
else {
        // the code to run if condition is false
}
```

Flowchart:

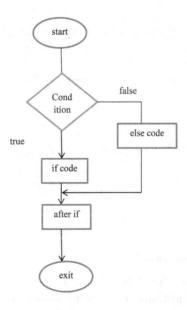

Statement of if-else.

Example:

```kotlin
fun main(args: Array<String>) {
        var a = 7
        var b = 13
        if(a > b){
            print("Number 7 is larger than 13")
        }
        else{
            println("Number 13 is larger than 7")
        }
    }
```

If-Else Expression in Kotlin as Ternary Operator

Because it returns a result, if-else may be used as an expression in Kotlin. In contrast to Java, there is no ternary operator in Kotlin since if-else returns the value based on the condition and operates just like ternary.

The Kotlin program to discover the bigger value between two integers using an if-else statement is shown below:

```kotlin
fun main(args: Array<String>) {
    var c = 70
    var d = 50

    // if-else returns value which is to be stored in
the max variable
    var max = if(c > d){
        print("The Greater number is: ")
        c
    }
    else{
        print("The Greater number is:")
        d
    }
    print(max)
}
```

If-Else-If Ladder Expression

A user can enter numerous criteria here. All of the "if" statements are performed. All of the conditions are examined one by one, and if any of them are found to be true, the code associated with the if statement is run, and all other statements are skipped until the end of the block. If none of the conditions are met, the last else statement is performed by default.

Syntax:

```
if(first-condition)
{
    // the code to run if condition is true
}
else if(second-condition)
{
    // the code to run if condition is true
}
else
{
}
```

Flowchart:

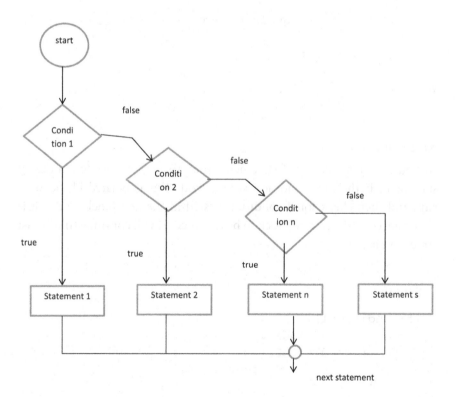

Statement of if-else-if.

The Kotlin program to determine whether a number is positive, negative, or equal to zero is shown below:

```kotlin
import java.util.Scanner
fun main(args: Array<String>) {
    // to create an object for scanner class
    val reader = Scanner(System.'in')
    print("Enter number: ")

    // to read the next Integer value
    var nums = reader.nextInt()
    var result   = if ( nums > 0){
        "$num is positive number"
    }
    else if( nums < 0){
        "$nums is negative number"
    }
    else{
        "$nums is equal to zero"
    }
    println(result)

}
```

Nested If Expression

Nested if statements are if statements that are nestled inside another if statement. If the first condition is true, code the associated block to be run, and then check for if condition nested in the first block, and if it is also true, code the related block to be executed. It will continue till the last condition is met.

Syntax:

```kotlin
if(condition1){
            // code-1
        if(condition2){
                // code-2
        }
    }
```

Flowchart:

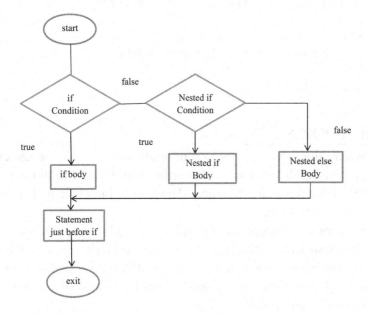

Statement of nested-if.

The Kotlin program to find the greatest value among three integers is shown below:

```kotlin
import java.util.Scanner
fun main(args: Array<String>) {

    // to create an object for scanner class
    val reader = Scanner(System.'in')
    print("Enter 3 numbers: ")
    var nums1 = reader.nextInt()
    var nums2 = reader.nextInt()
    var nums3 = reader.nextInt()
    var max  = if ( nums1 > nums2) {
        if (nums1 > nums3) {
            "$nums1 is the largest number"
        }
        else {
            "$nums3 is the largest number"
        }
    }
```

```
else if( nums2 > nums3){
    "$nums2 is the largest number"
}
else{
    "$nums3 is the largest number"
}
println(max)
}
```

WHILE LOOP IN KOTLIN

In programming, a loop is used to continually run a given code block until a condition is fulfilled. If you need to print a count from 1 to 100, you must repeat the print command 100 times. However, using a loop may save time and write only two lines.

While loops are consisting of a code block and a condition, the condition is first tested, and if true, the code within the block is run. It is repeated until the condition turns false since the condition is verified before entering the block each time. The while loop may be thought of as a series of if statements that are repeated.

Syntax of a while loop:

```
while(condition) {
        // the code to run
}
```

Flowchart:

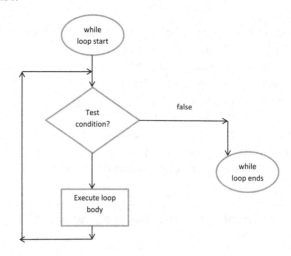

Statement of while-loop.

Using a while loop, this Kotlin program prints integers from 1 to 10: We use a while loop to display the numbers in the following program. First, set the variable numb to 1. Put the expression (numb = 10) in a while loop and check whether it is true or false. If true, it enters the block, executes the print statement, and increases the number by one. This process is repeated until the condition turns false.

```kotlin
fun main(args: Array<String>) {
    var numb = 1
    while(numb <= 10) {
        println(numb)
        numb++;
    }
}
```

Using a while loop, this Kotlin program prints the elements of an array: In the following program, we build an array (name) and initialize it with a different number of strings, and set a variable index to 0. array-Name.size may use to compute the size of an array. In the while loop, provide the condition (index < name.size).

If index value is less than or equal to the array size, it enters the block and prints the name stored at the corresponding index and increment the index value after each iteration. This process is repeated until the condition turns false.

```kotlin
fun main(args: Array<String>) {
    var name = arrayOf("Praniti","Gautam","Akashay","S
idharth","Abhinav","Manav")
    var index = 0
    while(index < name.size) {
        println(name[index])
        index++
    }
}
```

DO-WHILE LOOP IN KOTLIN

Do-while loops, like Java, are control flow statements that run a block of code at least once without verifying the condition, and then repeatedly execute the block, or not, depending entirely on a Boolean condition at the end of the do-while block. In contrast to the while loop, which runs the block only when the condition becomes true, the do-while loop performs the code first and then evaluates the expression or test condition.

Working of Do-While Loop

The condition is evaluated after all of the statements in the block have been executed. If the condition is met, the code block is re-executed. The code block execution procedure is repeated as long as the expression evaluates to true. If the expression becomes false, the loop exits, and control is transferred to the sentence after the do-while loop.

It is also known as a post-test loop as it tests the condition after the block has been executed.

The syntax of the do-while loop is as follows:

```
do {
        // the code to run
{
while(condition)
```

Flowchart:

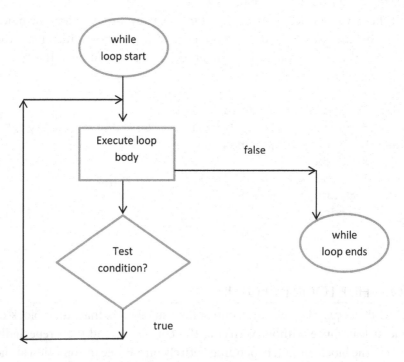

Statement of do-while-loop.

A Kotlin program that uses a do-while loop to calculate the factorial of a number:

```kotlin
fun main(args: Array<String>) {
    var numb = 6
    var factorial = 1
    do {
        factorial *= numb
        numb--
    }while(numb > 0)
    println("The Factorial of 6 is $factorial")
}
```

Program of printing a table of two using a do-while loop:

```kotlin
fun main(args: Array<String>) {
    var numb = 2
    var c = 1

    do {
        println("2 * $c = "+ numb * c)
        c++
    }while(c < 11)
}
```

FOR LOOP IN KOTLIN

The for loop in Kotlin is equivalent to the foreach loop in other languages such as C#. The for loop is used here to loop through any data structure that has an iterator. It is not used in the same way as the for loop in other programming languages such as Java or C.

The syntax of a for loop in Kotlin is as follows:

```kotlin
for(item in collection) {
    // the code to execute
}
```

The for loop in Kotlin is used to iterate over the following since they all offer an iterator:

- Range
- String

- Array

- Collection

Iterate across the Range Using a For Loop

Range offers an iterator so that we can traverse it. There are several ways to iterate across range. The in operator is used in the for loop to determine whether or not the value is within the range.

The following programs are examples of traversing the range in various ways, where in is the operator to verify the value in the range. If the value is between the ranges, it returns true and outputs the value.

Print the values when we iterate over the range:

```
fun main(args: Array<String>)
{
    for (c in 1..6) {
        print("$c ")
    }
}
```

Using step 3, iterate over the range to jump:

```
fun main(args: Array<String>)
{
    for (c in 1..10 step 3) {
        print("$c ")
    }
}
```

We can't iterate across range from top to down unless we use downTo:

```
fun main(args: Array<String>)
{
    for (c in 5..1) {
        print("$c ")
    }
    println("It print nothing")
}
```

Iterate over the range from top to down using downTo:

```
fun main(args: Array<String>)
{
    for (c in 5 downTo 1) {
        print("$c ")
    }
}
```

Iterate over the range from top to down using downTo, and then step 3:

```
fun main(args: Array<String>)
{
    for (c in 10 downTo 1 step 3) {
        print("$c ")
    }
}
```

Using a For Loop, Iterate over the Array

Array is a data-structure that holds data of the same kind, such as an integer or a string. Because it includes an iterator, an array may be traversed using a for loop. Each array has a beginning index, which is by default 0.

We can traverse the array in the following ways:

- Without using index property

- With using index property

- Using withIndex() library function

Without utilizing the index property, traverse an array:

```
fun main(args: Array<String>) {
    var numbs = arra
yOf(11,22,33,44,55,66,77,88,99,100)

    for (num in numbs) {
        if (num%2 == 0) {
            print("$num ")
        }
    }
}
```

Using the index property, traverse an array:

```kotlin
fun main(args: Array<String>) {
    var colors = arrayOf("Green", "Yellow", "Blue",
"Red", "White")
    for (i in colors.indices) {
        println(planets[i])
    }
}
```

Using the withIndex() library function, we may traverse an array:

```kotlin
fun main(args: Array<String>) {
    var colors = arrayOf("Green", "Yellow", "Blue",
"Red", "White")
    for ((index,value) in colors.withIndex()) {
        println("Element at $index th index is
$value")
    }
}
```

Iterate through a String Using the For Loop

Because the for loop includes an iterator, it may traverse a string.

The string can traverse in the following ways:

- Without using index property

- With using index property

- Using withIndex library function

```kotlin
fun main(args: Array<String>) {
    var name = "Hub"
    var name2 = "oftutors"
    // traversing the string without using index
property
    for (alphabets in name)   print("$alphabets ")
    // traversing the string with using index
property
    for (i in name2.indices) print(name2[i]+" ")
    println(" ")
    // traversing the string using withIndex()
library function
```

```
    for ((index,value) in name.withIndex())
        println("The Element at $index th index is
    $value")
    }
```

Iterate over the Collection Using the For Loop

The for loop may use to traverse the collection. Collections are classified into three types: List, Map, and Set.

We can pass different data types to the listOf() method at the same time.

The program to traverse the list using a for loop is shown below:

```
fun main(args: Array<String>) {
    // to read only, fix-size
    var collection = listOf(1,2,3,"listOf", "mapOf",
"setOf")
    for (elements in collection) {
        println(elements)
    }
}
```

WHEN EXPRESSION IN KOTLIN

Expression when replaces the switch operator of other languages such as Java in Kotlin. A specific block of code must be performed when a given condition is met. The when expression parameter compares each branch one by one until a match is found. When the first match is detected, it reaches the end of the when block and executes the code following the when block. We do not need a break statement at the end of each case, unlike a switch case in the Java or any other programming language.

When may be used in two ways in Kotlin:

- when as a statement

- when as an expression

When to Use as a Statement with Else

When may be used as a statement with or without the else branch. When used as a statement, the values of all individual branches are successively compared with the argument, and the relevant branch is executed when the condition matches. If none of the branches satisfy the requirement, the else branch is executed.

```
import java.util.Scanner;
fun main(args: Array<String>) {
    var reader = Scanner(System.'in')
    print("Enter largebody:")
    var lbt = reader.next()
    when(lbt) {
        "Sun" -> println("The Sun is a Star")
        "Moon" -> println("The Moon is a Satellite")
        "Earth" -> println("The Earth is a planet")
         else -> println("don't know anything")
    }
}
```

Using When as a Statement in the Absence of an Else Branch

We may use when as a statement in the absence of an otherwise branch. When used as a statement, the values of all individual branches are sequentially compared with the argument, and the relevant branch is executed when the condition matches. If none of the branches satisfy the requirement, the block simply departs without printing anything to the system output.

```
import java.util.Scanner;
fun main(args: Array<String>) {
    var reader = Scanner(System.'in')
    print("Enter-name:")
    var lbt = reader.next()

    when(lbt) {
        "Sun" -> println("The Sun is a Star")
        "Moon" -> println("The Moon is a Satellite")
        "Earth" -> println("The Earth is a planet")
    }
}
```

When Used as an Expression

If used as an expression, the value of the branch with which the condition is satisfied becomes the value of the overall expression. Using an expression produces a result that matches the parameter, which we may save in a variable or print directly.

```
import java.util.Scanner;
fun main(args: Array<String>) {
    var reader = Scanner(System.'in')
    print("Enter the month of number:")
    var monthyear = reader.nextInt()
    var months = when(monthyear)
{
        1->"Jan"
        2->"Feb"
        3->"March"
        4->"April"
        5->"May"
        6->"June"
        7->"July"
        8->"Aug"
        9->"Sept"
        10->"Oct"
        11->"Nov"
        12->"Dec"
        else -> {
            println("Not a month of the year")
        }
    }
println(months)
}
```

If the argument doesn't satisfy any of the branch requirements, the else branch is performed. The else branch is required as an expression, unless the compiler can demonstrate that all possible scenarios are handled by branch conditions. If we are unable to use the else branch, a compiler error will be generated.

Error:(7, 16) Kotlin: "when" expression must be exhaustive, add necessary "else" branch.

In Kotlin, Different Ways to Use When Block

We can use a comma to separate several branches in one. When some branches share common logic, we can unite them into a single branch. In the following example, we need to determine whether the entered largebody is a planet or not; therefore, we combined all planet names into a single branch. Anything different than the planet name will cause the else branch to be executed.

```
import java.util.Scanner;
fun main(args: Array<String>) {
    var reader = Scanner(System.'in')
    print("Enter the name of planet: ")
    var names = reader.next()
    when(names) {
        "Mercury","Earth","Mars","Jupiter",
            "Neptune","Saturn","Venus","Uranus" ->
println("Planet")
        else -> println("Neither the planet nor the
star")
    }
}
```

Check Whether the Input Value Is Inside the Range

We may verify the range of arguments supplied in when block using the in or !in operator. In Kotlin, the "in" operator is used to check for the existence of a certain variable or attribute within a range. If the argument lies inside a specific range, the in operator returns true; if the argument does not lies within a specific range, the !in operator returns true.

```
import java.util.Scanner;
fun main(args: Array<String>) {
    var reader = Scanner(System.'in')
    print("Enter month number of the year: ")
    var numb = reader.nextInt()
    when(numb){
        in 1..3 -> println("It is the spring season")
        in 4..6 -> println("It is the summer season")
        in 7..8 ->println("It is the rainy season")
        in 9..10 -> println("It is the autumn season")
        in 11..12 -> println("It is the winter
season")
        !in 1..12 ->println("Enter the valid month of
year")
    }
}
```

Check Whether a Provided Variable Is of a Specific Type

We may verify the type of variable passed as an input in the when block using the is or !is operator. If the variable is of the integer type, is Int returns true; otherwise, it returns false.

```
fun main(args: Array<String>) {
    var numb: Any = "Huboftutors"
    when(numb){
        is Int -> println("its an Integer")
        is String -> println("its a String")
        is Double -> println("its a Double")
    }
}
```

Using When as a Replacement for an If-Else-If Chain

When can be used in place of if-else-if. If no arguments are provided, the branch conditions are simply Boolean expressions, and a branch is performed only when its condition is true:

```
fun isOdd(c: Int) = c % 2 != 0
fun isEven(c: Int) = c % 2 == 0
fun main(args: Array<String>) {
    var numb = 8
    when{
        isOdd(numb) ->println("Odd")
        isEven(numb) -> println("Even")
        else -> println("neither even or not odd")
    }
}
```

Verify If a String Includes a Certain Prefix or Suffix

The method below may also use to check for a prefix or suffix in a supplied string. If the string has the prefix or suffix, it will return true; otherwise, it will return false.

```
fun hasPrefix(company: Any) = when (company) {
    is String -> company.startsWith("Huboftutors")
    else -> false
}
```

```
fun main(args: Array<String>) {
    var company = " Huboftutors a computer science
portal"
    var result = hasPrefix(company)
    if(result) {
        println("Yes, string started with
Huboftutors")
    }
    else {
        println("No, String does not started with
Huboftutors")
    }
}
```

UNLABELED BREAK IN KOTLIN

When working with loops, if we want to end the loop's execution instantly once a given condition is met, we may use either a break or a return expression to leave the loop.

This section will teach us how to utilize a break expression to quit a loop. When the break expression is encountered in a program, it returns to the nearest enclosing loop.

In Kotlin, there are two types of break expressions: unlabeled break expressions and labeled break expressions. We will learn how to utilize unlabeled break expressions in while, do-while, and for loops.

Use of Unlabeled Break in a While Loop

Unlabeled break is used to escape the loop without checking the test expression when it meets a certain condition. The control is then passed to the next while block statement.

Break syntax in a while loop:

```
while(test expression) {
        // the code to run
            if(break condition) {
                break
            }
        // the another code to run
}
```

A Kotlin program that computes the sum of integers from 1 to 10:

```
fun main(args: Array<String>) {
    var sum = 0
```

```
    var c = 1
    while(i <= Int.MAX_VALUE) {
        sum += c
        c++
        if(c == 11) {
            break
        }
    }
    print("sum of integers from 1 to 11: $sum")
}
```

In the above program, we use a while loop and a break expression to compute the sum of numbers from 1 to 10. Create a variable sum and set its initial value to 0. Iterate through the loop again, and this time set variable I to 1.

Iterator now proceeds from i = 1) and executes the sum statement. When the iterator value i reaches 11, the break expression is executed, and the loop is exited without testing the test expression i = Int.MAX VALUE). The control then goes to the while block's print() instruction, which prints the total of integers = 55.

Use of Unlabeled Break in a Do-While Loop

We may also use the break expression in a do-while loop to quit the loop without testing the test expression.

Break in a do-while loop syntax:

```
do {
    //the code to run
    if(break-condition) {
        break
    }
while(test-expression)
```

An array's elements are printed using a Kotlin program:

```
fun main(args: Array<String>) {
    var name = arrayOf("Earth","Mars","Venus","Jupiter
","Saturn","Uranus")
    var c = 0

    do{
        println("The name of $c th planet: "+name[c])
        if(name[c]=="Jupiter") {
            break
```

```
    }
    c++
  }while(c<=name.size)
}
```

We traverse the array in the preceding program to print the names of planets. First, initialize the array names with planet names, and i is the iterator for the test statement. We calculate size of an array using name. size.

The do block prints the array's element first, and then compares the array's value at any index to "Jupiter" every time. If it does match, increase the iterator and run one more. If the expressions match, the break expression is executed, and the do-while loop is terminated without checking for the test expression.

Use of Unlabeled Break in a For Loop

We can use a break expression when traversing a for loop within an array or string.

The syntax of break in for loop is as follows:

```
for(iteration through iterator) {
            // the code to run
      if(break-condition){
          break
      }
}
```

Kotlin program for printing a string up to a specific character: In the program below, we traverse the string to break at a specific position by comparing the char value. First, create an array with the name "Hubsoftutors" and the value "Hubsoftutors." Then a for loop with an iterator I to explore. It outputs the char value and compares it to char "s" at each point. The loop is terminated if a match is found, and control is transferred to the next statement.

```
fun main(args: Array<String>) {
    var name = "Hubsoftutors"
    for (c in name){
      print("$c")
            if(c == 's') {
```

```
            break
        }
    }
}
```

LABELED BREAK IN KOTLIN

Suppose we want to terminate the loop's execution instantly if a specific condition is met when interacting with loops. We may escape the loop by using either a break or a return expression in this situation.

In this tutorial, we'll look at utilizing a break expression to leave a loop. When the break statement is encountered in a program, it returns to the nearest enclosing loop.

In Kotlin, there are two sorts of break expressions: As we all know, unlabeled break is used to terminate to the nearest enclosing loop when a given condition is met.

However, a labeled break returns to a desired loop when a given condition is met. It is possible to accomplish this with the use of labels. Label is an identifier followed by a @ sign, such as inner@, outer@, first@, second@, and so on. Label can use with any expression, but it must be written in front of it.

We'll see how to employ labeled break expressions in while, do-while, and for loops.

Use of Labeled Break in a While Loop

When a certain condition is met, a labeled break is used to leave the target block without verifying the condition in the while loop. The control is then passed to the next statement of the while block.

If you use the label outer@ to identify the outer loop, we can simply break it using break@outer in the break condition block.

while loop labeled break syntax:

```
outer@ while(condition) {
    // code...
    inner@ while(condition) {
        // code...
        if(break-condition) {
            break @outer
        }
    }
}
```

Program of using labeled break in a while loop in Kotlin:

```kotlin
fun main(args: Array<String>) {
    var numb1 = 4
    outer@ while (numb1 > 0) {
        var numb2 = 4
        inner@ while (numb2 > 0) {
            if (numb1==2)
                break@outer
            println("numb1 = $numb1, numb2 = $numb2")
            numb2--
        }
        numb1--
    }
}
```

When the (num1 == 2) expression is true, the break@outer is performed, ending the desired loop marked with outer@.

Use of Labeled Break in a Do-While Loop

The labeled break is also run in the do-while loop to finish the desired loop. In this case, we've used outer@ for the outer do-while loop and inner@ for the inner do-while loop.

In a do-while loop, the syntax of a labeled break is as follows:

```kotlin
outer@ do {
    // code..
    inner@ do {
        // code..
        if(break-condition) {
            break@outer
        }
    } while(condition)
} while(condition)
```

Program of using labeled break in a do-while loop in Kotlin:

```kotlin
fun main(args: Array<String>) {
    var numb1 = 4
    outer@ do {
```

```
        var numb2 = 4
        inner@ do {
            if (numb1 == 2)
                break@outer
            println("numb1 = $numb1; numb2 = $numb2")
            numb2--
        } while (numb2 > 0)
        numb1--
    } while (numb1 > 0)
}
```

We print the same output as in the while loop here. When the (num1 == 2) expression is true, the break@outer command is performed, which ends the desired loop marked with outer@.

Use of Labeled Break in a For Loop

We can also use a labeled break to stop the desired loop if a given condition is met in the for loop. The outer for loop has been labeled as outer@, while the inside for loop has been labeled as inner@. Iteration in for loop is done using an iterator.

Labeled break in for loop syntax:

```
outer@ for(iteration through iterator) {
    // code..
        inner@ for(iteration through iterator)
            // code..
            if(break-condition) {
            break@outer
            }
        }
}
```

Kotlin program that employs a labeled break in a for-loop:

```
fun main(args: Array<String>) {
    outer@ for (numb1 in 4 downTo 1) {
        inner@ for (numb2 in 4 downTo 1) {
            if (numb1 == 2)
                break@outer
```

```
        println("numb1 = $numb1; numb2 = $numb2")
    }
  }
}
```

UNLABELED CONTINUE IN KOTLIN

In this section, we will learn how to utilize continue in Kotlin. When programming with loops, it is occasionally beneficial to skip the current iteration of the loop. In such a situation, we may utilize the program's continue statement. Continue is essentially used to repeat the loop for a given condition. It skips the following statements and moves on to the next loop iteration.

In Kotlin, there are two kinds of continues - unlabeled continue and labeled continue:

We'll see at how to utilize unlabeled continue in while, do-while, and for loops.

Use of Unlabeled Continue in a While Loop

In Kotlin, the unlabeled continue is used to skip current iteration of the nearest enclosing while loop. If condition for continue is true, it skips the instructions after continue and returns to the beginning of the while loop. It will check for the condition again, and the loop will repeat until it becomes false.

The syntax of an unlabeled continue in a while loop is as follows:

```
while(condition) {
    //code...
      if(condition for continue) {
      continue
      }
    //code...
}
```

Flowchart:

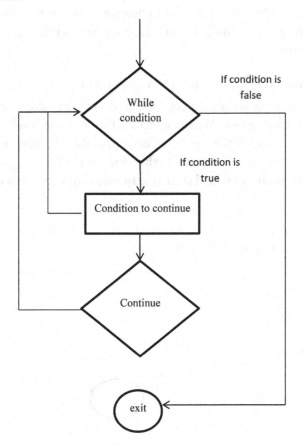

unlabeled continue in a while loop.

The continue in while loop is used in a Kotlin program:

```kotlin
fun main(args: Array<String>) {
    var numb = 0
    while (numb <= 15) {
        if (numb % 3 == 0) {
            numb++
            continue
        }
        println(numb)
        numb++
    }
}
```

In the preceding program, we print the integers and skip all multiples of 3. The phrase (num % 3 == 0) is used to determine if a number is divisible by 3. If the number is a multiple of three, increase it without printing it to standard output.

Use of Unlabeled Continue in a Do-While Loop

We may also use the unlabeled continue in do-while to skip the iteration of the nearest closing loop. We must include the continue condition in the do block in this case. If the condition becomes false, the next instruction will skip, and control will transfer to the while condition.

The syntax of an unlabeled continue in a do-while loop is as follows:

```
do{
     // code...
     if(condition for continue) {
     continue
     }
}
while(condition)
```

Flowchart:

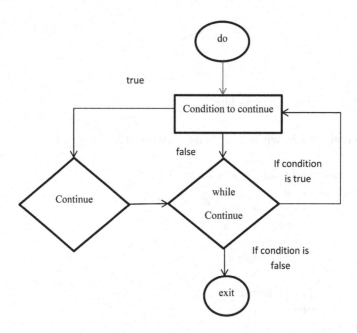

unlabeled continue in a do-while loop.

Kotlin program to utilize continue in a do-while loop:

```
fun main(args: Array<String>) {
    var numb = 1
    do {
        if (numb <= 5 || numb >=15) {
            numb++
            continue
        }
        println("$numb")
        numb++
    } while (numb < 20)
}
```

We used the condition (num = 5 || num >=15) in the preceding program to skip printing numbers to the standard output less than or equal to 5 and more than or equal to 15. As a result, it only prints the digits 6–14.

Use of Unlabeled Continue in a For Loop

We can also use unlabeled continue in for loop to skip the current iteration to the closing loop. We used an array of letters and an iterator to traverse the array planets in the following program. The equation (i < 2) skips iterating through array indices less than two; therefore, it does not display the text stored at indexes 0 and 1.

The following is the syntax for an unlabeled continue in a for loop:

```
for(iteration through iterator)
{
    //code..
    if(condition for continue)
{

    continue
    }
}
```

Flowchart:

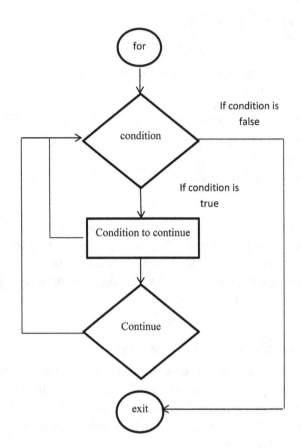

Kotlin program to use continue in for loop:

```kotlin
fun main(args: Array<String>) {
    var colors = arrayOf("Green", "Yellow", "Blue",
"White", "Orange")
    for (i in colors.indices) {
        if(i < 2){
            continue
        }
        println(colors [i])
    }
}
```

LABELED CONTINUE IN KOTLIN

In this topic, we will learn how to utilize continue in Kotlin. It is occasionally beneficial to skip the current loop iteration when dealing with a loop in programming. In such a situation, we may utilize the program's continue statement. Continue is essentially used to repeat the loop for a given condition. It skips the following statements and moves on to the next loop iteration.

In Kotlin, there are two forms of continuing.

Unlabeled continue, as we know, skips the iteration of the nearest closing loop, whereas labeled continue skips the iteration of the intended closing loop. It may be done with the use of labels such as inner@, outer@, and so on. We put a label in front of the phrase and call it with continue@abc.

Use of Labeled Continue in a While Loop

In the while loop, labeled continue is used to skip the iteration of the desired block when it meets a specified condition without checking the condition in the while loop. If we mark the outside loop with outer@ and the inner loop with inner@, you can simply skip for the specified condition in the conditional block by using continue@outer.

The syntax for labeled continue in a while loop is as follows:

```
outer@ while(first-condition) {
    // code…
    inner@ while(second-condition) {
        //code…
        if(condition for continue) {
            continue@outer
        }
    }
}
```

Kotlin program that uses labeled continue in a while loop:

```
fun main(args: Array<String>) {
    var numb1 = 4
    outer@ while (numb1 > 0) {
        numb1--
        var numb2 = 4
        inner@ while (numb2 > 0) {
            if (numb1 <= 2)
                continue@outer
```

```
        println("numb1 = $numb1, numb2 = $numb2")
        numb2--
    }
  }
}
```

Use of Labeled Continue in a Do-While Loop

In the do-while loop, we may also utilize the designated continue. We utilized a nested do-while loop in the following program, labeling the outside loop with outer@ and the inner loop with inner@. The continue condition is executed within an inner do-while loop. If the condition is true, continue@outer skips the next lines or expressions and returns control to outer do-while for repetition.

In the do-while loop, the syntax for labeled continue is as follows:

```
outer@ do {
    // code...
    inner@ do {
        // code...
        if(condition for continue) {
            continue@outer
        }
    } while(first-condition)
} while(second-condition)
```

Kotlin program that uses labeled continue in a do-while loop:

```
fun main(args: Array<String>) {
    var numb1 = 4
    outer@ do {
        numb1--
        var numb2 = 4
        inner@ do {
            if (numb1 <= 2)
                continue@outer
            println("numb1 = $numb1; numb2 = $numb2")
            numb2--
        } while (numb2 > 0)

    } while (numb1 > 0)
}
```

Use of Labeled Continue in a For Loop

In addition, we may utilize labeled continue in for loop. We utilized nested for loops in the following program, labeling the outside loop with outer@ and the inner loop with inner@. The continue condition is executed within the inner for-loop. If the condition is met, the next statements are skipped, and the control is passed to the outer for-loop for further iteration.

The syntax for labeled continue in for loop is as follows:

```
outer@ for(iteration through iterator) {
    // code..
        inner@ for(iteration through iterator) {
            // code..
            if(condition for continue) {
            continue@outer
            }
        }
}
```

Kotlin program that uses for loop with a continue label:

```
fun main(args: Array<String>) {
    outer@ for (numb1 in 4 downTo 1) {
        inner@ for (numb2 in 4 downTo 1) {
            if (numb1 <= 3)
                continue@outer
            println("numb1 = $numb1; numb2 = $numb2")
        }
    }
}
```

CONCLUSION

This chapter covered the control flow statement where we learned if-else, while loop, do-while loop, and for loop. Moreover, we covered when expression, labeled and unlabeled break, and labeled and unlabeled continue.

CHAPTER 5

Arrays and Strings, Functions, and Java Interoperability

IN THIS CHAPTER

➤ Array and String

➤ Functions

➤ Recursion and Expression

➤ Calling Kotlin from Java

In Chapter 4, we covered control flow statements in Kotlin. In this chapter, we will cover array and string, functions that include lambda expressions, recursion, and inline functions. Moreover, we will also learn about how to call Kotlin from Java.

ARRAYS IN KOTLIN

The array data structure is one of the most fundamental data structures in almost all computer languages. Array is a data-structure that allows us to store several items of the same data type, such as integer or string, under a single variable name.

Arrays are used in programming to arrange data so that a related group of values can be readily sorted or searched.

DOI: 10.1201/9781003311904-5

Arrays have the following basic properties:

- They are kept in memory in contiguous memories.
- Their indexes allow them to be accessed programmatically (array[1], array[0], etc.).
- They are malleable.
- Their sizes are fixed.

Creation of an Array

Arrays are not native data types in Kotlin, but rather a mutable collection of related items represented by the Array class.

In Kotlin, an array may define in two ways.

Making Use of the arrayOf() Function

By passing values of elements to the library function arrayOf(), we may generate an array.

Syntax:

```
val numb = arrayOf(1, 2, 3, 4)    //type
declaration implicit
val numb = arrayOf<Int>(1, 2, 3) //type
declaration explicit
```

Program of creating the array using arrayOf() and arrayOf<Int> functions:

```
fun main()
{
    // declarion of array using arrayOf()
    val arrayname = arrayOf(11, 22, 33, 44, 55)
    for (c in 0..arrayname.size-1)
    {
        print(" "+arrayname[c])
    }
    println()
    // the declarion of an array using arrayOf<Int>
    val arrayname2 = arrayOf<Int>(1, 2, 3, 4, 5)
```

```
for (c in 0..arrayname2.size-1)
{
    print(" "+arrayname2[c])
}
}
```

Making Use of the Array Constructor

Because array is a class in Kotlin, we can also create an array using the Array constructor.

The constructor accepts two parameters:

- The array's size.

- A function that accepts the index of a given element and returns its initial value.

Syntax:

```
val numb = Array(3, {c-> c*1})
```

In the above example, we pass the array's size as 3 and a lambda function that initializes element values from 0 to 9.

Program of creating array using constructor:

```
fun main()
{
    val arrayname = Array(5, { c -> c * 1 })
    for (c in 0..arrayname.size-1)
    {
        println(arrayname[c])
    }
}
```

Aside from these, Kotlin provides various built-in factory methods for creating arrays of primitive data types like byteArray, intArray, shortArray, and so on. Although they implement the same methods and attributes, these classes do not extend the Array class.

The factory method for creating an integer array, for example:

```
val numb = intArrayOf(1, 2, 3, 4)
```

Other factory methods for creating arrays include:

- byteArrayOf()

- charArrayOf()

- shortArrayOf()

- longArrayOf()

Array Access and Modification

So far, we've covered how to build and initialize an array in Kotlin. Let's look at how to access and modify them now.

There are two options:

- **Using the get() and set() Functions:** As you may be aware, an array in Kotlin is essentially a class. As a result, we may access a class object's data using its member functions. The methods get() and set() are referred to as member functions.

  The get() function accepts a single parameter, the element's index, and returns the item's value at that index.

  First Syntax:

  ```
  val x = numb.get(0)
  ```

  The set() function accepts two parameters: the element's index and the value to insert.

  Second Syntax:

  ```
  num.set(1, 3)
  ```

  The above code sets value of the array's second element to 3.

- **Using the index operator [ ]:** Arrays can access and modify using the [] operator.

  The syntax for accessing an array element would be:

  ```
  val x = numb[1]
  ```

  This will set x to the value of the second element in numb.

To change an array element, we must perform the following:

```
numb[2] = 5;
```

The value of the third element in the numb array will change to 5.

Note that the index operator, or [], is an overloaded operator that only stands for calls to the get() and set() member functions.

Here's an example of Kotlin array manipulation in action, in which we build an array, edit its values, and access a specific element:

```
fun main()
{    // declare an array using arrayOf()
     val numb = arrayOf(1, 2, 3, 4, 5)

     numb.set(0, 10)  // set first element equal to 10
     numb.set(1, 6)   // set secondelement equal to 6

     println(numb.get(0)) // print first element
using get()
     println(numb[1]) // print second element using []
}
```

Array Traversal

An array's key quality is that it can traverse programmatically, and each element in the array may change separately. Kotlin provides a few useful methods for traversing arrays.

The for-loop is the simplest and most often used idiom for traversing an array.

First Syntax:

```
for(c in numb.indices){
     println(numb[c])
   }
```

Kotlin array traversal program using for loop:

```
// traversing an array
fun main()
{
    val numb = arrayOf<Int>(1, 2, 3, 4, 5)
```

```
numb.set(0, 10)
numb.set(1, 6)
for (c in numb.indices)
{
    println(numb[c])
}
}
```

To get the same result, we may also utilize the range. A range in Kotlin is an interval between two values (start and finish) that may create with the (..) operator. The in keyword may then use to traverse the range.

Range syntax is as follows:

```
for (c in 0..10){
    println(c)
}
```

An array's element range is defined as 0 to size-1. So, to traverse an array using the range, we execute a loop on the array name from 0 to size-1.

Program of an array traversal in Kotlin using range:

```
// traversing an array
fun main()
{
    val arraynames = arrayOf<Int>(1, 2, 3, 4, 5)
    for (c in 0..arraynames.size-1)
    {
        println(arraynames[c])
    }
}
```

The forEach loop is another, probably less time-consuming, approach to perform the above.

Second Syntax:

```
arraynames.forEach({index->println(index)})
```

Program of an array traversal using forEach loop:

```
// traversing an array
fun main()
```

```
{
    val arraynames = arrayOf<Int>(1, 2, 3, 4, 5)
    arraynames.forEach({ index -> println(index) })
}
```

STRING IN KOTLIN

A string is an array of characters. Kotlin strings are comparable to Java strings; however, they include several additional features. Kotlin strings are likewise immutable, which implies that we cannot modify the components or length of the string.

In Kotlin, the String class is defined as follows:

```
class string : Comparable<String>, Char-Sequence
```

In Kotlin, we must use double quotes (" ") to declare a string; single quotes are not permitted to define strings.

Syntax:

```
var variable_name = "Hello, Everyone"
```

or

```
var variable_name : String = "Huboftutors"
```

Creation of an Empty String

To create an empty string, we must first create an instance of the String class.

```
var variable_name = String()
```

Templates and String Elements

- **String elements**

    A character, digit, or other symbols in a string is referred to as an element of a string. Using string[index], we can quickly get the element of the string. Elements are stored in a string starting at index 0 and ending at (string.length – 1).

    In Kotlin, string elements may access in three ways:

    - **Using index:** This method returns the character at the specified index.

- **Using the get function:** Returns the character at the specified index, which was passed as an input to the get function.

- **Iterating through the string:** To access the characters in the string, use loops.

To access the elements of a string in Kotlin, use the following code:

```
fun main(args: Array<String>) {
    // access the string elements one by one
    var str = "Hiiii"
    println(str[0])
    println(str[1])
    println(str[2])
    println(str[3])
    println(str[4])
    // access the string elements using for loop
    var str2 = "Everyone"
    for(c in str2.indices) {
        print(str2[c]+" ")
    }
}
```

- **String Template**
  String template expressions are evaluated pieces of code, and the results are delivered as strings. Template expressions can found in both escaped and raw string types. String templates begin with a dollar sign $ and are followed by either a variable name or an arbitrary expression enclosed in curly braces.

```
fun main(args: Array<String>) {
    var num = 10
    println("The value of n is $num")
    // using string
    val str = "Everyone"
    println("$str is string which length is ${str.
length}")
}
```

The string has the following essential properties and functions:

- **Length:** It returns the length of string.

```
var st =" String"
println(st.length)
```

- **get(index):** It returns the character at that particular index.

  ```
  st.get(3) // Output: - i
  ```

- **subSequence(start, end):** It returns a substring starting at the beginning and ending but excluding the end.

  ```
  st.subSequence(1, 4) // Output: - tri
  ```

- **str.compareTo(string):** It returns 0 if str == string.

  Kotlin program using the mentioned properties and functions:

  ```
  fun main(args: Array<String>) {
      var g1 = "PeeksForPeeks"
      var e1 = "Peeks"
      println(g1.length)
      println(g1.get(4))
      println(g1.subSequence(0, 5))
      println(g1.compareTo(e1))
  }
  ```

String Literals

In Kotlin, there are two kinds of string literals:

- Escaped string

- Raw string

Escaped String

An escape string is defined with double quotes ("....") and may contain escape characters such as /n, /t, and so on.

Escaped string Kotlin program:

```
fun main(args: Array<String>) {
    // the escaped string
    val str1 = "World \n is \n beautiful"
    println(str1)
}
```

Raw String – Multiline String

The raw string is enclosed in triple quotes ("""....""") and lacks escape characters. Because it allows us to split the string into numerous lines, it's also known as a multiline string.

Raw string Kotlin program:

```kotlin
fun main(args: Array<String>) {
// the raw string - multiline string
    var str1 = """My
        |name
        |is
        |Harsh
    """.trimMargin()
    println(str1)
}
```

Escape Characters

Some of the escapees include:

- **\"** : for double quote

- **\b** : for backspace

- **\n** : for newline

- **\'** : for single quote

- **\r** : for carriage return

- **** : for backslash

- **\t** : for tab

String Equality

Kotlin includes comparing instances of a specific type in two separate ways. This characteristic distinguishes Kotlin from other programming languages.

There are two kinds of equality:

- Structural equality

- Referential equality

Structural Equality

The = = operator and its inverse, the != operator, assess structural equality. The expression x==y is converted into a call to the type's equals() method by default.

Referential Equality

In Kotlin, referential equality is tested using the = = = operator and its opposite, the != = operator. This equality returns true only if two instances of the same type refer to the same memory location. When used on types that are converted to primitives at runtime, the = = = check is converted to = = check, and the != = check is converted to != check.

Program to demonstrate the structural and referential equality:

```
fun main(args: Array<String>) {
    var a = "PeeksForPeeks"
    var b = "PeeksForPeeks"
    var c = "Peeks"
    println(a= = =b) // true,   as both are pointing to
same StringPool
    println(a= =c) //false since values are not equal
    println(a= = =c) //false
}
```

FUNCTIONS IN KOTLIN

Function is a piece of code that does a specific task. Functions are used in programming to divide code into smaller modules, making the program more manageable.

For instance, if we need to compute the sum of two numbers, we may create a fun sum ().

```
fun sum(c: Int, d: Int): Int {
    return c + d
}
```

We may call sum(c, d) many times as we like, and it will always return the sum of two values. As a result, the function minimizes code repetition and makes code more reusable.

There are two kinds of functions in Kotlin:

- Standard library function

- User-defined function

Standard Library Function in Kotlin

In Kotlin, there are various built-in functions already specified in the standard library and ready to use. We can call them by passing parameters based on the situation.

We will utilize the built-in methods arrayOf(), sum(), and println() in the following program. To build an array, the method arrayOf() requires various arguments such as integers, double, and so on, and we can determine the total of all items using sum(), which does not require any inputs.

```kotlin
fun main(args: Array<String>) {
    var sum1 = arrayOf(1,2,3,4,5,6,7,8,9,10).sum1()
    println("Sum of all elements of an array is:
$sum1")
}
```

In the following program, we will use rem() to calculate the remainder:

```kotlin
fun main(args: Array<String>) {
    var numb1 = 26
    var numb2 = 3
    var result = numb1.rem(numb2)
    println("The remainder when $numb1 is divided by
$numb2 is: $result")
}
```

The following is a list of some standard library functions and their use:

- **sqrt():** This function is used to compute the square root of an integer.

- **print():** This function prints a message to standard output.

- **rem():** Returns the remainder of one number after it has been divided by another.

- **toInt():** This function converts a number to an integer value.

- **readline():** This function is used for standard input.

- **compareTo():** A function that compares two integers and returns a Boolean value.

Kotlin User-Defined Function

A user-defined function is one that the user defines. As we all know, to partition a huge program into little modules, we must first define the function. Each defined function has its own set of attributes, such as the function's name, the type of function's return value, the number of arguments passed to the function, and so on.

Defining user-defined functions: In Kotlin, functions may be declared at the top, eliminating the requirement to build a class to house a function, as we are used to doing in other languages such as Java or Scala.

In general, we define a function as follows:

```
fun fun_name(x: data_type, y: data_type, ......):
return_type  {
    // other code..
    return
}
```

- **fun:** A function-definition keyword.

- **fun name:** The function's name that will be used to call the function later.

- **a: data type:** Here, **a:** is a passed argument, and data type specifies the data type of the argument, such as integer or string.

- **return type:** This parameter specifies the type of data value returned by the function.

- **{....}:** Curly braces represent the function block.

To multiply two numbers with the same kind of arguments, use the Kotlin method mul():

```
fun mul(numb1: Int, numb2: Int): Int {
    var numbers = numb1.times(numb2)
    return numbers
}
```

Explanation: Above, we defined a function using the fun keyword whose return type is an integer.

```
>> The function's name is mul()
>> numb1 and numb2 are the names of the parameters
taken by the function, and they are both of the
integer type.
```

The Kotlin method student() has many sorts of parameters:

```
fun students(names: String,  roll_no: Int,  grades:
Char) {
    println("The Name of the students is : $names")
    println("The Rollno of the students is: $roll_no")
    println("The Grade of the students is: $grades")
}
```

Explanation: We defined a function with the fun keyword, with a return type of unit by default.

```
>> students is the function's name.
>> names is a string data type argument.
>> roll no is an integer data type parameter.
>> grades is a character data type parameter.
```

Calling a User-Defined Function

We write a function to do a certain activity. When a function is called, the program exits the current code section and starts executing the function.

A function's flow control:

- The program reaches the line containing a function call.

- When a function is called, control is passed to that function.

- Executes all of the function's instructions one by one.

- Only when the function reaches the closing braces or a return statement is control returned.

- Any function data returned is utilized in place of the function in the original line of code.

Program to call the mul() function by passing two arguments:

```
fun mul(c: Int, d: Int): Int {
    var number = c.times(d)
    return number
```

```
}
fun main(args: Array<String>) {
    var result = mul(4,6)
    println("Multiplication of 2 numbers is: $result")
}
```

Explanation: We call the mul(4, 6) function with two arguments in the above program. When the function is called, control is passed to mul(), which begins the execution of the statements in the block. It computes the multiple of two integers and stores the result in a variable number using the built-in times() function. The function then returns the integer value and controls transfer back to main(), where it calls mul(). The value produced by the function is then stored in the mutable variable result, and println() prints it to the standard output.

Program to call the student() method with all arguments:

```
fun students( names: String,  grades: Char,  roll_no:
Int) {
    println("The Name of the students is : $names")
    println("The Grade of the students is: $grades")
    println("The Rollno of the students is:
$roll_no")

}
fun main(args: Array<String>) {
    val name = "Pariniti"
    val rollno = 23
    val grade = 'C'
    students(names,grades,rollno)
    students("Gautam",'C',25)
}
```

Explanation: In the above program, we call the students() method by giving the parameters in the same order. When we try to jumble the parameters, we get a type mismatch error. In the first call, we use variables to provide the argument, and in the second call, we pass the parameter values without storing them in variables. As a result, both methods are valid for calling a function.

DEFAULT AND NAMED ARGUMENTS IN KOTLIN

Most programming languages require us to declare all of the parameters that a function takes when calling that function, but one of the most significant characteristics of Kotlin is that we do not need to specify all of the arguments that a function accepts when calling that function. We may remove this requirement and make parameters optional, allowing us to choose whether or not to give an argument when calling a function.

Function arguments in Kotlin are separated by comma and defined using Pascal notation, i.e., name:data_type.

```
fun fun_names(names1: data_type, names2: data_type)
```

In Kotlin, there are two kinds of arguments:

- Default arguments

- Named arguments

Default Arguments in Kotlin

The parameters that do not need to be specified explicitly when invoking a function are referred to as default arguments.

If function is called without any arguments, the function's default arguments are utilized as parameters. If arguments are given during a function call, they are utilized as function parameters in other circumstances.

There are three scenarios in which default parameters are used:

- No arguments are passed while calling a function

- Partial arguments are passed while calling a function

- All arguments are passed while calling a function

No Arguments Are Passed While Calling a Function

When no arguments are given when calling a function, the function parameters are the default arguments. While defining a function, we must initialize the variables.

Program for calling the students() method in Kotlin without supplying any parameters:

```
// the default arguments in the function definition
names, standard and roll_no
```

```
fun students(names: String="Praniti", standard:
String="IX",  roll_no: Int=11) {
    println("The Name of the students is: $names")
    println("The Standard of the students is:
$standard")
    println("The Roll no of the students is:
$roll_no")
}
fun main(args: Array<String>) {
    val names_of_students = "Gautam"
    val standard_of_students = "VII"
    val roll_no_of_students = 23
    students()            // passing no arguments while
calling the students
}
```

Explanation: In the preceding program, we utilized the student function, which takes three arguments: names, standard, and roll no. It's worth noting that we've assigned a value to each of the student's parameters. It is used to guarantee that these are the default settings if no arguments are passed into the students() function when calling the function. As a result, because no arguments are supplied in the preceding program, it uses the default arguments as function parameters and outputs the default values to standard output.

Partial Arguments Are Passed While Calling a Function
Some of the arguments given when calling a function are utilized as function parameters here. The default value will utilize if a formal argument does not get a value from the function call.

Kotlin program that calls the students() method and passes certain parameters:

```
// default arguments in function definition
names,standard and roll_no
fun students( names: String="Praniti", standard:
String="X",  roll_no: Int=13 ) {
    println("The Name of the students is: $names")
    println("The Standard of the students is:
$standard")
    println("The Roll no of the students is:
$roll_no")
}
```

```
fun main(args: Array<String>) {
    val names_of_students = "Gautam"
    val standard_of_students = "VII"
    val roll_no_of_students = 24
    // passing only two arguments name and standard of
students
    students(names_of_students,standard_of_students)
}
```

Explanation: In the preceding program, we utilized the student function, which takes three arguments: names, standard, and roll no. It's worth noting that we've assigned a value to each of the student's parameters. We passed data for the student's name and standard here. As a result, for roll no, it will utilize the default value (13) and display all of the values to standard output.

All Arguments Are Passed While Calling a Function
In this case, we must pass all of the parameters defined in the function declaration, but the data type of the real arguments must match the data type of the formal arguments in the same sequence.

    Kotlin program for calling the students() method with all parameters:

```
// the default arguments in function definition names,
standard and roll_no
fun students( names: String="Praniti", standard:
String="X",  roll_no: Int=13 ) {
    println("The Name of the students is: $names")
    println("The Standard of the students is:
$standard")
    println("The Rollno of the students is: $roll_no")
}

fun main(args: Array<String>) {
    val names_of_students = "Gaurav"
    val standard_of_students = "VIII"
    val roll_no_of_students = 25

    //passing all the arguments of the students name,
    //standard and roll_no in the same order as
defined in function

students(names_of_student,standard_of_students,roll_
no_of_students)
}
```

Explanation: In the preceding program, we gave all of the arguments to the students() function, which overwrites the default values for the function parameters. As a result, it only prints the values passed to formal arguments during the function call.

Named Arguments in Kotlin

We run into difficulty while working with the default arguments. If we jumble the arguments, a compilation error will occur; thus, we must provide the actual arguments to the formal arguments in the same order as defined in the function definition.

Kotlin program for executing students() with parameters passed in random order:

```kotlin
// the default arguments in the function definition
names,standard and roll_no
fun students( names: String="Praniti", standard:
String="X",  roll_no: Int=13 ) {
    println("The Name of the students is: $names")
    println("The Standard of the students is: $standard")
    println("The Roll no of the students is:
$roll_no")
}

fun main(args: Array<String>) {
    val names_of_students = "Gautam"
    val standard_of_students = "VII"
    val roll_no_of_students = 23
    // passing the argument names_of_students to name
    // and roll_no_of_students to standard
    students(names_of_students,roll_no_of_students)
}
```

In the preceding program, we did not send the parameters in the order stated in the function. As a result, it returns a compilation error.

Named arguments are parameters that are supplied using the name while calling a function. We must use name of the formal argument to which we are passing the actual argument value when calling the function.

Program for calling students() with the following arguments:

```kotlin
// the default arguments in the function definition
// names,standard and roll_no
```

```
fun students( names: String="Praniti", standard:
String="X",  roll_no: Int=13 ) {
    println("The Name of the students is: $names")
    println("The Standard of the students is:
$standard")
    println("The Rollno of the students is: $roll_no")
}

fun main(args: Array<String>) {
    val name_of_students = "Gautam"
    val standard_of_students = "VII"
    val roll_no_of_students = 23

    // passing arguments with the name as defined in
function

students(names=names_of_students,roll_no=roll_no_of_
students)
}
```

Explanation: In this case, we used the name to pass the actual arguments to the formal arguments. We just gave the values for name and roll no; therefore, it prints the default value of "Students standard."

RECURSION IN KOTLIN

We will learn how to use the Kotlin recursive function. In Kotlin, we may utilize recursion just like in other programming languages.

A recursive function calls itself, and the act of recurrence is known as recursion.

When a function is called, one of two things is possible:

- Normal function call

- Recursive function call

Normal Function Call

When a function is called from the main() block, it is referred to as a regular function call. In the following example, sum() is called one at a time, and it runs its instructions before returning the sum of the numbers. If we wish to rerun the code, we must call sum() from the main block once again.

Calling the sum() function from main() block:

```
fun sum(a:Int, b:Int) : Int {
Val numb = a+b
return numb
}
fun main( args: Array < String>) {
sum()
}
```

Recursive Function Call

When a function calls itself, this is referred to as a recursive function call. Every recursive function should include a terminate condition, or otherwise, the program would enter an infinite loop, resulting in a stack overflow error.

Calling the callMe() function from its own block:

```
fun callMe(a:Int) {
println(a)
if (a > 0) callMe(a - 1)
}
fun main (args: Array <String>) {
var n  = 5
callMe()
```

In this case, we utilized the terminate condition if (a > 0); otherwise, it enters an infinite loop. It also prints the value from 5 to 0.

First Example: Determine the factorial of a number without using a terminate condition

```
// program of factorial using recursion
fun Fact(numb: Int):Long{
    return  numb*Fact(numb-1)  // no terminate
condition
}
//the main method
fun main() {
    println("The Factorial of 5 is: "+Fact(5))
//recursive-call
}
```

Second Example: Using the terminate condition; get the factorial of a number

```
// program of factorial using recursion
fun Fact(numb: Int):Long{
    return if(numb==1) numb.toLong()
// terminate-condition
    else numb*Fact(numb-1)
}
//the main method
fun main() {
    println("The Factorial of 5 is: "+Fact(5))
//recursive-call
}
```

Third Example: Using recursion, get the sum of an array's elements

```
// two parameters passed an array and the size of
array
fun sum(args: Array<Int>,  index:Int ):Int{
    return if(index<=0) 0
    else (sum(args, index-1) + args[index-1])
// recursive-function call
}
fun main() {
    // array-initialization
    val array = arrayOf(11,22,33,44,55,66,77,88,
99,100)
    // size of array
    val ny = array.size
    val result = sum(array,nu)
// normal function call
    println("Sum of array elements is: $result")
}
```

Explanation: We've initialized an array and provided it as an argument to the sum() method. The index value is decremented by one in each recursive call. If the index is zero or less, the program is terminated and the total of all the elements is returned.

TAIL RECURSION IN KOTLIN

In a traditional recursion call, we perform our recursive call first, then take the recursive call's return value and compute the result. In tail recursion, however, the computation is performed first, followed by the recursive call, with the results of the current step being sent to the next recursive call. In the end, both recursion and tail recursion provide the same result.

The must-follow rule for tail recursion is that the recursive call should be the method's final call.

Benefits of Employing Tail Recursion

- In tail recursion, the function call is the last item done by the function, and there is nothing left to run in the current function. As a result, there is no need to save the current function call in stack memory, and the compiler can reuse that stack space for the next recursive call.

- StackOverflowError does not occur during program execution in tail recursion.

First Example: Using tail-recursion, calculate the factorial of a number

```
// program of factorial using tail-recursion
fun Fact(numb: Int, x:Int):Long{
    return if(numb==1)    // terminate-condition
        x.toLong()
    else
        Fact(numb-1,x*numb)    //tail-recursion
}
fun main() {
    var n = 1
    var result = Fact(5,n)
    println("The Factorial of 5 is: $result")
}
```

Second Example: Using tail-recursion, calculate the sum of an array's elements

```
// two parameters passed an array and the size of
an array
```

```kotlin
fun sum(args: Array<Int>,  index:Int, s : Int = 0
):Int{
    return if(index<=0) s
    else sum(args, index-1, s + args[index-1])
// tail-recursion
}
fun main() {
    // array-initialization
    val array = arrayOf(1,2,3,4,5,6,7,8,9,10)
    // size of array
    val nu = array.size
    val result = sum(array,nu)                //
normal-function call
    println("Sum of array elements is: $result")
}
```

Explanation: In this case, we gave the array as an argument to the sum() method, along with two additional arguments. The (s) parameter's default value is zero. With each recursive call, we calculate the sum of the items starting at the last index of the array. We'll have the sum of all items in "s" with the final recursive call and return it when the condition is met.

LAMBDA EXPRESSIONS AND ANONYMOUS FUNCTIONS IN KOTLIN

This topic will cover lambda expressions and anonymous functions in Kotlin. While they are syntactically similar, Kotlin and Java lambdas have vastly distinct characteristics.

Lambdas expression and anonymous function are both function literals, which imply they are not declared but are supplied as an expression.

Lambda Expressions

As we all know, the syntax of Kotlin lambdas is quite similar to that of Java lambdas. An anonymous function does not have a name. We may call lambda expressions anonymous functions.

First Example:

```kotlin
fun main(args: Array<String>) {
    val company = { println("PeeksforPeeks")}
    // invoking the function method1
    company()
```

```
    // invoking the function method2
    company.invoke()
}
```

Syntax:

```
val lambda_names : Data_type = { argument_List ->
code_body }
```

Curly braces always enclose a lambda expression, argument declarations are enclosed by curly braces and have optional type annotations, and an arrow -> sign encloses the code body. If the lambda's inferred return type is not Unit, the final expression inside the lambda body is considered the return value.

Second Example:

```
val sum = {x: Int,  y: Int -> x + y}
```

Except for the code body, the lambda expression in Kotlin has optional parts. The lambda expression is shown below after the optional component has been removed.

```
val sum:(Int,Int) -> Int = { x, y -> x + y}
```

It's worth noting that we don't always need a variable because it can be supplied directly as an argument to a method.

Program:

```
// with the type annotation in lambda expression
val sum1 = { x: Int, y: Int -> x + y }
// without type annotation in lambda expression
val sum2:(Int,Int)-> Int  = { x,  y -> x + y}
fun main(args: Array<String>) {
    val result1 = sum1(1,4)
    val result2 = sum2(2,5)
    println("Sum of two numbers is: $result1")
    println("Sum of two numbers is: $result2")
    // directly print return value of the lambda
    // without storing in variable.
    println(sum1(4,6))
}
```

Inference in Lambda Types

Type inference in Kotlin assists the compiler in determining the type of a lambda expression. The lambda expression used to compute the sum of two numbers is shown below.

```
val sum = {x: Int,  y: Int -> x + y}
```

In this case, the Kotlin compiler evaluates it as a function that takes two Int parameters and returns an Int value.

```
(Int,Int) -> Int
```

If we want to return a String value, we may use the inbuilt function toString() method.

```
val sum1 = { x: Int, y: Int ->
    val num = x + y
    num.toString()      //convert the Integer to String
}
fun main(args: Array<String>) {
    val result1 = sum1(12,7)
    println("Sum of two numbers is: $result1")
}
```

The Kotlin compiler self-evaluates the preceding program into a function that accepts two integer values and returns a string.

Type Declaration in Lambdas

The type of our lambda expression must be explicitly declared. If lambda does not return a value, we can use: Unit.

```
Pattern: (Input) -> Output
```

Lambdas examples with return type:

```
val lambda1: (Int) -> Int = (x -> x * x)
val lambda2: (String,String) -> String = { x,  y -> x
+ y }
val lambda3: (Int)-> Unit = {print(Int)}
```

Lambdas can be used as class extension:

```
val lambda4: String.(Int) -> String = {this + it}
```

It represents implicit name of single parameter.

Program when lambdas used as class extension:

```kotlin
val lambda4 : String.(Int) -> String = { this + it }
fun main(args: Array<String>) {
    val result = "Peeks".lambda4(40)
    print(result)
}
```

Explanation: The preceding example uses the lambda expression as a class extension. We used the format mentioned above to pass the parameters. This keyword is used for string and the Int parameter given in the lambda. The code body then concatenates both values and returns to the variable result.

It: Implicit Name of a Single-Parameter
In most cases, lambdas only have one parameter. It is used here to indicate the single parameter passed to the lambda expression.

Program utilizing lambda function shorthand:

```kotlin
val numb = arrayOf(1,-2,3,-4,5)
fun main(args: Array<String>) {
    println(numb.filter { it > 0 })
}
```

Program with lambda function in longhand:

```kotlin
val numb = arrayOf(1,-2,3,-4,5)
fun main(args: Array<String>) {
    println(numb.filter {item -> item > 0 })
}
```

Returning a Value from a Lambda Expression
The final value returned by lambda expression after execution. The lambda function can return any integer, string, or Boolean values.

Kotlin program that uses a lambda function to return a String value:

```kotlin
val find =fun(numb: Int): String{
if(numb % 2==0 && numb < 0) {
    return "The number is even and negative"
  }
```

```
    else if (numb %2 ==0 && numb >0){
    return "The number is even and positive"
    }
    else if(numb %2 !=0 && numb < 0){
    return "The number is odd and negative"
    }
    else {
    return "The number is odd and positive"
    }
}
fun main(args: Array<String>) {
    val result = find(112)
    println(result)
}
```

Anonymous Function

An anonymous function is quite similar to a regular function except for the omission of the function's name from the declaration. The anonymous function's body can be either an expression or a block.

First Example: Function body as an expression

```
fun(x: Int, y: Int) : Int = x * y
```

Second Example: Function body as a block

```
fun(x: Int, y: Int): Int {
    val mul = x * y
    return mul
}
```

Return Type and Parameters

The return type and parameters are also supplied in the same way as regular functions, although the parameters can be omitted if they can be deduced from the context.

If the function is an expression, the return type can be deduced automatically from the function; otherwise, the anonymous function must explicitly provide a body block.

Distinction between Lambda Expressions and Anonymous Functions

The only difference is how non-local returns behave. A return statement without a label always returns from the function declared function.

This implies that a return within a lambda expression returns from the enclosing function, but a return within an anonymous function returns from the anonymous function itself.

Program to call the anonymous function:

```
// the anonymous function with body as an expression
val anonymous1 = fun(a: Int, b: Int): Int = a + b

// the anonymous function with body as a block
val anonymous2 = fun(x: Int, y: Int): Int {
                val mul = x * y
                return mul
                }
fun main(args: Array<String>) {
    //invoking functions
    val sum = anonymous1(13,4)
    val mul = anonymous2(5,6)
    println("Sum of two numbers is: $sum")
    println("Multiply of two numbers is: $mul")
}
```

INLINE FUNCTIONS IN KOTLIN

Higher-order functions or lambda expressions in Kotlin are all stored as objects; therefore, memory allocation for both function objects and classes, as well as virtual calls, may impose runtime costs. By inlining the lambda expression, we may sometimes reduce the memory overhead. To decrease the memory cost of such higher-order functions or lambda expressions, we may use the inline keyword, which instructs the compiler not to create memory and simply copy the inlined code of that function to the calling place.

Example:

```
fun higherfunc( str1 : String, mycall :(String)->
Unit) {
    // invokes print() by passing the string str1
    mycall(str1)
}

// the main function
fun main(args: Array<String>) {
```

```
    print("Huboftutors: ")
    higherfunc("A Computer Science portal for
Hub",::print)
}
```

Bytecode: Because Kotlin, like Java, is a platform-independent language, it first translates to bytecode. The bytecode may obtain by selecting Tools -> Kotlin -> Show Kotlin Bytecode. Decompile to obtain this bytecode.

The main part to pay attention to in the preceding bytecode is:

```
mycall.invoke(str1)
```

By passing the string as an argument, mycall calls the print function. Invoking print() would result in an additional call, increasing memory overhead.

It functions as follows:

```
mycall(new-Function() {
        @Override
        public void invoke() {
          //the println statement is called here.
        }
    });
```

If we call large number of functions as arguments, each of which adds to the method count, there is a significant impact on memory and speed.

In the preceding program, what will the inline keyword do?

```
inline fun higherfunc( str1 : String, mycall :
(String)-> Unit){
    // invokes print() by passing the string str1
    mycall(str1)
}
// main function
  fun main(args: Array<String>) {
    print("Hunoftutors ")
    higherfunc("A Computer Science portal for
Hub",::print)
  }
```

The println lambda expression is copied in the main function in the form of System.out.println with the assistance of the inline keyword, and no additional calls are necessary.

Non-Local Control Flow

If we want to return from lambda expression in Kotlin, the Kotlin compiler does not allow it. We may use the inline keyword to return from the lambda expression and exit the function called the inlined function.

Program of using return in a lambda expression in Kotlin:

```
var lambda = { println("Lambda-expression")
              return }         // normally lambda
expression doesn't allow return
                      // statement, so gives
compile-time error
fun main(args: Array<String>) {
    lambda()
}
```

Normally, it does not permit returning from lambda and returns an error.

```
var lambda1 = { println("Lambda-expression")}
fun main(args: Array<String>) {
    lambda1()
}
```

Normally, everything functions great without it, and the statement is printed.

Kotlin program for using return in lambda and passing as an argument to an inlined function:

```
fun main(args: Array<String>){
    println("The Main function starts")
    inlinedFunc({ println("Lambda-expression 1")
    return },       // inlined function allows return
                    // statement in the lambda
expression
                    // so, doesn't give the compile
time error
```

```
    { println("Lambda expression 2")} )

    println("The Main function ends")
}
    // The inlined function
inline fun inlinedFunc( lmbd1: () -> Unit, lmbd2: ()
-> Unit  ) {
    lmbd1()
    lmbd2()
}
```

Explanation: We called the inlinedFunc() method with two lambda phrases as parameters. We send both as parameters to the inlined function when we call it from the main function. In the inlined code, lmbd1() called the first expression, and the return keyword causes the lambda expression and the main function from which it was called to depart.

Crossline Keyword

Return in lambda in the preceding program exits both the inline function and enclosing function. To stop the lambda expression from returning, we can use the crossline. If it encounters a return statement in the lambda expression, it will generate a compiler error.

Example:

```
fun main(args: Array<String>){
    println("The Main function starts")
      inlinedfunc({ println("Lambda-expression 1")
        return },      // It gives the compiler
error
          { println("Lambda-expression 2")} )

    println("The Main function ends")
}
inline fun inlinedfunc( crossinline lmbd1: () ->
Unit, lmbd2: () -> Unit  ) {
    lmbd1()
    lmbd2()
}
```

Noinline

If we want part of the lambdas passed to an inline function to inline, we may use the noinline modifier on some of the function arguments.

```
fun main(args: Array<String>){
    println("The Main function starts")
    inlinedFunc({ println("Lambda-expression 1")
        return },     // It doesn't compiler time
error
        { println("Lambda-expression 2")
            return } )     // It gives the compiler
error
    println("The Main function ends")
}
inline fun inlinedFunc( lmbd1: () -> Unit, noinline
lmbd2: () -> Unit  ) {
    lmbd1()
    lmbd2()
}
```

Reified Type Parameters

Sometimes we need to know what parameter was passed during the call. We pass the argument when calling the function, and we can obtain the parameter type using a reified modifier.

```
fun main(args: Array<String>) {
    genericFunc<String>()
}
inline fun <reified D> genericFunc() {
    print(D::class)
}
```

Properties of Inline

Inlined functions copy the code to the calling location, while inline keywords copy the inline property accessor methods to the calling location. The inline modifier can use to property accessors that do not have a backing field.

```
fun main(args: Array<String>) {
    print(flag)
}
```

```
fun foo(x: Int ): Int{
    var c = x
    return c
}
inline var flag : Boolean
    get() = foo(10 ) == 10
    set(flag) {flag}
```

INFIX FUNCTION NOTATION IN KOTLIN

In this topic, we'll go over the infix notation that's utilized in Kotlin functions. A function tagged with the infix keyword in Kotlin can also be called using infix notation, which implies calling without the need of parentheses and dots.

In Kotlin, there are two forms of infix function notation:

- Standard library infix function notation

- User-defined infix function notation

Standard Library Infix Function Notation

When we use operators, like and, or, shr, shl, and so on, the compiler looks for the function and calls the one we want. There are other standard library infix notation methods; however, we will cover a few of them here.

Let's go over some of the infix notations one by one.

1. **Kotlin program that uses bitwise and operator:**

   ```
   fun main(args: Array<String>) {
       var x = 14
       var y = 11
       var z = 10
       // call using dot & parenthesis
       var result1 =(x > y).and(x > z)
       println("The Boolean result1 = $result1")
       // call using infix notation
       var result2 =(x > y) and (x > z)
       println("The Boolean result1 = $result2")
   }
   ```

   Explanation: We used infix to call the x.and(y) method here (x and y).

   In the standard output, both provide the same result.

2. **Kotlin program that employs the signed shift right (shr) operator:**

```
fun main(args: Array<String>) {
    var x = 8
    // // call using infix notation
    var result1 = x shr 2
    println("Signed shift right by 2 bit:
$result1")
    // call using the dot and parenthesis
    var result2 = x.shr(1)
    println("The Signed shift right by 1 bit:
$result2")
}
```

Explanation: In the preceding program, we utilized a signed shift operator. First, use infix notation to operate, followed by dot and parentheses.

If we signed shift the value by two bits, we get 2(3–2=1) =2.

3. **A Kotlin program that employs the increment and decrement operators:**

```
fun main(args: Array<String>) {
    var x = 8
    var y = 4

    println(++x)        // call using the infix
notation
    println(x.inc())    // call using the dot and
parenthesis
    println(--y)        // call using the infix
notation
    println(y.dec())    // call using the dot and
parenthesis
}
```

Explanation: We utilized increment and decrement operators in infix notation in this case.

++x signifies x(8) + 1, resulting in a print of 9.

x.inc() also represents x(9) + 1; therefore, it outputs 10, whereas y represents y(4) – 1 = 3.

y.dec() represents y(3) – 1 = 2 as well.

Notation for User-Defined Infix Functions

We can write our own functions in infix notation if they meet the following criteria:

- It must be a member or extension function.

- It must only take one argument.

- The parameter cannot take a variable number of inputs and has a default value.

- It must be prefixed with the keyword infix.

Program to create a square function in Kotlin using infix notation:

```kotlin
class maths {
    // the user defined infix member function
    infix fun square(x : Int): Int{
        val num = x * x
        return num
    }
}
fun main(args: Array<String>) {
   val y = maths()
   // the call using infix notation
   val result = y square 3
   print("The square of a number is: "+result)
}
```

Explanation: In the preceding program, we constructed our own infix notation function (y square 3).

1. First and foremost, we defined the infix notation function within a maths class since it must be a member function.

2. The infix keyword is used to identify the function.

3. It has one parameter and no default value, and the function return type is similarly integer.

   ```kotlin
   square(x : Int):Int
   ```

Then, we created an object for the class maths() and invoked the method using infix notation.

```
y square 3
```

It squares the number and returns the result 9.

Kotlin program to verify the data type of a variable using infix notation:

```
class checks{
    // the user defined infix member function
    infix fun dataType(a: Any):Any{
    var x = when(a){
            is String -> "String"
            is Int -> "Integer"
            is Double -> "Double"
            else -> "invalid"
        }
        return x
    }
}
fun main(args: Array<String>){
    var chk = checks()
    // call using infix notation
    var results = chk dataType 3.3
    println(results)
}
```

Explanation: To determine the data type of a variable, we constructed an infix notation function.

The data type was supplied as a parameter in the infix call:

```
chk dataType 3.3
```

when the data type of the passing argument is checked, and the required result is returned.

It returns double to the standard output in this case.

Infix Function Precedence over Operators

When it comes to the execution of an instruction, precedence is essential. Infix function calls come after arithmetic operators, type casts, and the rangeTo operator.

The following expressions are equivalent:

```
2 shr 1 + 2 and 2 shr (1 + 2)
1 until m * 2 and 0 until (m * 2)
xs union ys as Set<*> and xs union (ys as Set<*>)
```

On the other hand, Infix function calls take priority over the Boolean operators && and ||, is- and in-checks, and several other operators.
The following expressions are also equivalent:

```
x xor y || z and a xor (y || z)
 x in y xor z and a in (y xor z)
```

HIGHER-ORDER FUNCTIONS IN KOTLIN

The Kotlin programming language provides excellent support for functional programming. Kotlin functions can be kept in variables and data structures, and they can be passed as parameters to and returned from higher-order functions.

Higher-Order Function

Higher-Order functions in Kotlin are functions that can receive a function as an argument or return a function. We shall pass anonymous functions or lambdas instead of passing integer, string, or array as function parameters. Lambdas are frequently passed as parameters in Kotlin functions for simplicity.

The lambda expression is passed as an argument to the higher-order function: A lambda expression can be passed as a parameter to higher-order function.

There are two kinds of lambda expressions that may be passed:

- A lambda expression returns a unit.

- Lambda expression returns any of the values integer, string, and so on.

Kotlin lambda expression program that returns Unit:

```
// lambda expression
var lambda = {println("Huboftutors: A Computer Science
portal for Hub") }
        //the higher-order function
fun higherfunc( lmbd: () -> Unit ) {        // accepting
lambda as parameter
```

```
    lmbd()                                      //invokes the
lambda expression
}
fun main(args: Array<String>) {
    //invoke higher-order function
    higherfunc(lambda)                     // passing the
lambda as parameter
}
```

Explanation: Let's go over the above program step by step.

In the top, we define a lambda expression that includes print() to print a string to standard output.

```
var lambda = {println("Huboftutors: A Computer Science
portal for Hub") }
```

After that, we define a higher-order function with one parameter.

```
lmbd: () -> Unit
```

- The receiving lambda parameter is known locally as lmbd.

- The symbol () indicates that the function does not accept any parameters.

- The unit symbol symbolizes that the function does not return any value.

- We called the higher-order function in the main function by supplying the lambda expression as a parameter.

  ```
  higherfunc(lambda)
  ```

Kotlin lambda expression program that returns an integer value:

```
    // lambda expression
var lambda = {x: Int,  y: Int -> x + y }
    // the higher order function
fun higherfunc( lmbd: (Int, Int) -> Int) {        //
accepting the lambda as parameter

    var results = lmbd(2,4)     // invokes lambda
expression by passing parameters
```

```
    println("Sum of two numbers is: $results")
}

fun main(args: Array<String>) {
    higherfunc(lambda)              //passing lambda as
parameter
}
```

Explanation: Let's go over the program above step by step.
At the top, we define a lambda expression that returns an integer value.

```
var lambda = int x, int y -> x + y
```

Then we defined a higher-order function that takes the lambda expression as an argument.

```
lmbd: (Int, Int) -> Int
```

- The receiving lambda argument is known locally as lmbd.

- (Int,Int) indicates that the function accepts two integer parameters.

- Int indicates that the function returns an integer value.

We called the higher-order function in the main function by passing the lambda as a parameter.

```
higherfunc(lambda)
```

Passing a function as a parameter to a higher-order function: a function can be passed as a parameter to a higher-order function.
There are two kinds of functions that may be passed:

- method that returns Unit

- function that returns any of the values integer, string, and so on.

Kotlin function passing program that returns Unit:

```
// the regular function definition
fun printMe(s1:String): Unit{
    println(s1)
}
```

```
    // the higher-order function definition
fun higherfunc( str1 : String, myfunc: (String) ->
Unit){
    // invoke the regular function using local name
    myfunc(str1)
}
fun main(args: Array<String>) {
    // invoke the  higher-order function
    higherfunc("Huboftutors: A Computer Science portal
for Hub",::printMe)
}
```

Explanation: At the top, we build a normal method printMe(), which receives a string parameter and returns a Unit.

```
fun printMe(s1:String): Unit
```

- (s1: String) is the only parameter

- Unit represents the return type

The higher-order function is thus defined as:

```
fun higherfunc( str1 : String, myfunc: (String) ->
Unit)
```

It is given two parameters. One is the string type, and the other is the function.

- **Str1:** String denotes a string parameter.

- **myfunc:** (String) -> Unit indicates that it accepts function as a parameter and returns Unit.

The higher function is invoked from the main function by supplying the string and function as arguments.

```
higherfunc("Huboftutors: A Computer Science portal for
Hub",::printMe)
```

Program of passing function which returns integer value:

```kotlin
// the regular function definition
fun add(x: Int, y: Int): Int{
    var sums = x + y
    return sums
}
    //the higher-order function definition
fun higherfunc(addfunc: (Int,Int)-> Int){
    // invoke the regular function using local name
    var results = addfunc(13,6)
    print("The sum of two numbers is: $results")
}
fun main(args: Array<String>) {
    // invoke the higher-order function
    higherfunc(::add)
}
```

Returning a Function from a Higher-Order Function

A function can return from a higher-order function. When returning the function, we must define the normal function's argument types and return type in the higher-order function's return type.

Program of a function in Kotlin that returns another function:

```kotlin
// the function declaration
fun mul(x: Int, y: Int): Int{
    return x*y
}
    //the higher-order function declaration
fun higherfunc() : ((Int,Int)-> Int){
    return ::mul
}
fun main(args: Array<String>) {
    // invoke the function and store the returned
function into a variable
    val multiply = higherfunc()
    // invokes the mul() function by passing arguments
    val results = multiply(12,4)
    println("Multiplication of two numbers is:
$results")
}
```

JAVA INTEROPERABILITY – USING JAVA TO CALL KOTLIN

Kotlin was designed to function alone on the JVM; therefore, it has a comprehensive set of features that make calling Kotlin from Java. Kotlin class objects, for example, can be readily generated, and their methods may call from Java methods. However, there are certain guidelines for using Kotlin code in Java.

Properties of Kotlin

In Java, a property is defined as a private field with the same name as the property and a getter and setter method, with get and set prefixed to the property name. This private field may be found in the java class created from the Kotlin file.

In Java, for example, the property var age: Int is compiled to the following code:

```
private int ages;
public int getAge(){
  return ages;
}
public void setAge(int ages){
  this.ages = value;
}
```

These attributes may be accessed via the class's object, much like in Java. If the property name begins with is, the get keyword is skipped from the getter function's name.

Package-Level Functions

All Kotlin functions declared within a package are compiled into static Java methods within a class whose classname is a mixture of the package name and the filename.

For example, suppose there is a package named kotlinPrograms and a Kotlin file called firstex.kt that has the following code.

```
// The Kotlin file
package kotlinPrograms
class myprogram {
  fun add(val x:Int, val y:Int): Int {
   return x+y;
  }
}
```

In Java, use the following syntax to call this function:

```
// Java
new kotlinPrograms.firstex.myClass()
kotlinPrograms.Firstexkt.add(3, 5);
```

Using the @JvmName annotation, we may alter the name of the produced Java class:

```
// Kotlin file
@file : Jvmname("Samples")
package kotlinPrograms

class myclass {
  fun add(val x:Int, val y:Int): Int {
    return x+y;
  }
}
```

In Java, use the following syntax to call this function:

```
// Java
new kotlinPrograms.firstex.myClass()
kotlinPrograms.Samples.add(3, 5);
```

Having numerous files with the same name, on the other hand, is a logical mistake. To overcome this limitation, Kotlin gives its compiler the ability to generate a façade class with a specific name containing all declarations from all files with the same name. To develop such a facade class, provide the annotation @JvmMultiFileClass in all files.

Example:

```
// Kotlin code
@file:JvmName("Samples")
@file:JvmMultiFileClass
package samples.example
fun print(){.......}
```

Another Kotlin file:

```
// Kotlin code
@file:JvmName("Samples")
@file:JvmMultiFileClass
```

```
package samples.example
fun printString(){.......}
```

In Java, both of these methods may be called using the following syntax:

```
// Java calling statements
samples.example.Samples.print()
samples.example.Samples.printString()
```

Static Fields

In Java, static fields are properties specified within a named object or a companion object in Kotlin. To access these fields in Java, they must be annotated with the @JvmField annotation, defined with the lateinit modifier, or annotated with the const modifier.

Example:

```
// filename Example.kt
// Property in companion object
class xyz{
 companion object{
      @JvmField
      val a = 4;
  }
}
// A constant property
const val b = 4;
```

Static Methods

Methods declared at the package level are always created in the Java code as static methods. Methods specified in named objects and companion objects annotated with @Jvm are also included. Static annotations are created in the same way as static methods are. This annotation indicates that the following method is a class function.

Example:

```
// filename Example.kt
class xyz {
  companion object {
```

```
@JvmStatic fun add(val x:Int, val y:Int):Int{
   return x+y;
   }
 fun sub(val x:Int, val y:Int):Int{
   return x-y;
   }
  }
}

//Java usage
xyz.add(); // works fine
xyz.sub(); // error: not a static method
xyz.Companion.add(); // instance method remains
Z.Companion.sub(); // the only way it works
```

Instance Fields

Kotlin has a feature that allows us to utilize the property as an instance field in Java. Annotate the property with the @JvmField annotation to do this. The visibility of these instance fields is the same as that of the Kotlin property. The property, however, must have a backing field and cannot be defined with the private, open, const, or override modifiers.

Example:

```
// Kotlin code
class XYZ(z: Int){
 @JvmField val id = z
}
```

This property is now accessible in Java as:

```
XYZ obj = new XYZ(5);
System.out.println(obj.id);
```

Checked Exceptions

In Kotlin, all exceptions are unchecked. As a result, the Java signatures of Kotlin functions never declare nor handle the exceptions that are thrown. To address this issue, the Kotlin function must be annotated with the @Throws annotation, which specifies the exception that will be thrown. The Java signature will also declare the function that will throw in this instance.

Example:

```
// samples Kotlin function
// filename example.kt
package Samples
fun print(){
 throws IOException()
}
```

```
// Java code trying to call the above  function
try {
    Samples.Example.print();
    }
    // This statement causes error because it does
not declare IOexception in throws list
    catch(IOException e) {
}
```

So, in order to address the error, we declare the @Throws annotation at the beginning.

```
// Overcoming problem with @Throws annotation
package Samples
@Throws(IOException::class)
fun print()
{
throws IOException()
}
```

JAVA INTEROPERABILITY – USING KOTLIN TO CALL JAVA

Kotlin was designed with interoperability with Java in mind. It facilitates the usage of Java code from within itself. In a simple way, a Kotlin class or function can relate to Java classes and methods.

Getters and Setters in Java

In Kotlin, the getters and setters of all types declared within the Java class are represented as properties. As a result, to access the getters and setters of a Java class's data members, it must be referenced as a property within Kotlin.

example.java is a Java file that has been declared:

```java
// the Java class
public class example {
  private int values;
  public int getValue(){
      return values;
  }
  public void setValue(int values){
      this.values = values;
  }
}
```

Kotlin file declared as kotlinexample.kt

```kotlin
// Kotlin file
fun main(){
   val ob = example()
   ob.values = 5 // This will call the setter function
   println(ob.values) // This will call the getter
function
}
```

Methods

Calling Java methods from within Kotlin is a simple idea. The arguments to be given are the same in both Java and Kotlin, as is the function's return type. The void return type is the lone exception to this rule. In Kotlin, functions with a void return type in Java return a Unit type. Because Unit is a type in Kotlin, this value may store.

Java file declared as example.java:

```java
// Java code
public class program {
    public int add(int c, int d){
        return c+d;
    }
}
```

Kotlin file declared as kotlinexample.kt:

```kotlin
// Kotlin file
fun main(args: Array<String>) {
```

```
    val ob = myjava()
    val ans = ob.add(14, 4)
    println("Sum of two numbers is "+ans)
}
```

Note: Some Kotlin keywords may be used as valid identifiers in Java. For instance, any, sealed, object, and so on. If this is the case, use identifiers in Kotlin, enclosing them in a backtick character (').

For instance, if a Java class ABC has a method named any, the method may be invoked in Kotlin as:

```
ob.'any'() // ob is the instance of the class ABC
```

Static Members

In Kotlin, the static class members become the members of a companion object. These companion objects, however, cannot be utilized directly in expressions. To gain access to its members, utilize the member's fully qualified name as defined in Java.

Java file declared as example.java:

```
// Java Code
package mypackage;
    public class example {
    public static void display() {
        System.out.println("Call-successful")
    }
}
```

Kotlin file declared as kotlinexample.kt:

```
// declare kotlin package
  package myktpackage
  // import java class using java package
  import mypackage.example
  fun main(args: Array<String>) {
      // calling the static member of java class
      val str1 = example.display()
      println(str1)
  }
```

Java Arrays

In contrast to Java arrays, which may be assigned to an array of type Object, Kotlin offers an invariant form of arrays, which means that arrays of a certain type cannot give to an array of type Any.

Furthermore, arrays of subclass types cannot be assigned to arrays of superclass types in Kotlin.

Because Kotlin does not provide arrays for primitive types, it offers numerous specialized classes in Java to represent an array of primitive kinds. These classes are unrelated to the Array class, and they are compiled into simple java arrays for optimum speed. This conversion to bytecode adds no additional cost, regardless of how the arrays are utilized.

Java file declared as example.java:

```
// Java Code
public class example {
    int results = 0;
    public int compute(int[] array)
    {
        for(int x: array){
            results = result + x;
        }
        return results;
    }
}
```

Kotlin file declared as kotlinexample.kt:

```
// Kotlin-code
fun main(args: Array<String>) {
    // Kotlin-code
    val ob = example()
    val array = intArrayOf(11, 22, 33, 44, 55, 66)
    var sum1 = ob.compute(array)
    println("The sum of an array is "+sum1)
}
```

Java Varargs

In functions, Java supports the concept of variable-length arguments, which means that when the number of arguments to a function is unknown but their type is known, we define a varargs parameter. Kotlin does not accept varargs arguments but, in order to be completely functional with Java, it offers a specific spread operator (*) to call methods that do.

Java file declared as example.java:

```java
// Java code
public class example {
    public void myfunc(String str1,int... numbers) {
        System.out.println("Passed string is " +
str1);
        for (int nu : numbers) {
            System.out.print(" "+nu);
        }
    }
}
```

Kotlin file declared as kotlinexample.kt:

```kotlin
// Kotlin code
fun main(args: Array<String>) {
    val ob = example()
    val array = intArrayOf(12, 21, 13)
    ob.myfunc("Peeks", *array)
}
```

Types in Java and Kotlin Are Not the Same

Types in Kotlin are not the same as types in Java. Kotlin, on the other hand, offers a mapping from Java types to Kotlin types in order to maintain interoperability. This mapping occurs at build time, and no noticeable difference in speed is observed at runtime.

The following primitive types are mapped to Java primitive types:

Java Type	Kotlin Type
Byte	kotlin.Byte
Short	kotlin.Short
Java Type	Kotlin Type
Int	kotlin.Int
Long	kotlin.Long
Char	kotlin.Char
Float	kotlin.Float
Double	kotlin.Double
Boolean	kotlin.Boolean

Some of the java.lang package's built-in classes are also mapped to Kotlin classes:

Java Type	Kotlin Type
java.lang.Object	kotlin.Any!
java.lang.Cloneable	kotlin.Cloneable!
java.lang.Comparable	kotlin.Comparable!
java.lang.Enum	kotlin.Enum!
java.lang.annotation	kotlin.Annotation!
java.lang.CharSequence	kotlin.CharSequence
java.lang.String	kotlin.String!
java.lang.Number	kotlin.Number!
java.lang.Throwable	kotlin.Throwable!

In Kotlin, the boxed types of Java's primitive data types are mapped to nullable types:

Java Type	Kotlin Type
java.lang.Byte	kotlin.Byte?
java.lang.Short	kotlin.Short?
java.lang.Integer	kotlin.Int?
java.lang.Long	kotlin.Long?
java.lang.Character	kotlin.Char?
java.lang.Float	kotlin.Float?
java.lang.Double	kotlin.Double?
java.lang.Boolean	kotlin.Boolean?

CONCLUSION

In this chapter, we covered array and string in Kotlin, functions where we also covered inline, infix function, tail recursion, and lambda expressions. Moreover, we covered Java interoperability.

CHAPTER 6

Collections in Kotlin

IN THIS CHAPTER

➢ Collection

➢ ArrayList, listOf, setOf

➢ HashSetOf

➢ Map, HashMap

➢ Annotations, Reflection, Overloading

➢ Tuple in Kotlin

In Chapter 5, we covered array and string, function, and Java interoperability. This chapter will cover collection with ArrayList, listOf, setOf, and MutableSet.

COLLECTIONS IN KOTLIN

Kotlin, like Java Collections, introduces the idea of collections. A collection often comprises a number of objects of the same type, referred to as elements or items in the collection. The Kotlin Standard Library provides a complete set of utilities for managing collections.

Types of Collections

Collections in Kotlin are classified into two types:

1. Immutable Collection

2. Mutable Collection

DOI: 10.1201/9781003311904-6

Immutable Collection

It signifies that it only provides read-only functionality and that its elements cannot edit. Immutable collections and their associated techniques are as follows:

- **List:** listOf() and listOf<T>()

- **Set:** setOf()

- **Map:** mapOf()

List   It is an ordered collection in which we may access elements or objects by utilizing indices – integer numbers that determine each element's position. Elements in a list can be repeated an unlimited number of times. We can't add or remove items from the immutable list. The following Kotlin program demonstrates the immutable list:

```
// example for the immutable list
fun main(args: Array<String>) {
    val immutableLists =
listOf("Mahi","Nikita","Ruhi")
    // gives the compile-time error
    // immutableLists.add = "Praniti"
    for(item in immutableLists){
        println(item)
    }
}
```

Set   It is an unordered collection of elements that does not support duplicate elements. It is a collection of one-of-a-kind components. In general, the order of set components has no major influence. Because it is an immutable Set, we cannot execute add or remove operations. The following Kotlin program demonstrates the immutable set:

```
fun main(args: Array<String>) {
    // initialize with the duplicate values
      // but the output with no repetition
    var immutableSets = setOf(7,8,8,1,0,"Mahi",
"Nikita")
    // gives the compile time error
    // immutableSets.add(7)
```

```
for(item in immutableSets){
    println(item)
}
}
```

Map   Each key in a Map is unique and holds just one value; it is a set of key-value pairs. Each key corresponds to a single value. Values can duplicate, but keys must be distinct. Maps are used to store logical link between the two things such as a student's ID and name. Its size is fixed since it is immutable, and its methods provide read-only access. The following Kotlin application demonstrates the immutable Map:

```
// example for immutable map
fun main(args : Array<String>) {
    var immutableMaps = mapOf(9 to "Mahi",8 to
"Nikita",7 to "Ruhi")
    // gives compile time error
    // immutableMaps.put(9,"Praniti")
    for(key in immutableMaps.keys){
        println(immutableMaps[key])
    }
}
```

Mutable Collection
It has both read and write capabilities. Mutable collections and their associated techniques are as follows:

- **List:** mutableListOf(), arrayListOf(), and ArrayList

- **Set:** mutableSetOf() and hashSetOf()

- **Map:** mutableMapOf(), hashMapOf(), and HashMap

List   Because mutable lists may be read and written to, defined elements in the list can be deleted or added. The following Kotlin program demonstrates the mutable list:

```
fun main(args : Array<String>) {
    var mutableLists = mutableListOf("Mahl","Nikita","
Ruhi")
    // we can modify the element
```

```
mutableLists[0] = "Praniti"
// add one more element in list
mutableLists.add("Abhi")
for(item in mutableLists){
    println(item)
}
}
```

Set   The mutable Set allows for both read and write operations. We may simply add or delete elements from the collections, and the order of the components is preserved. To show the mutable set, write the following Kotlin program:

```
fun main(args: Array<String>) {
    var mutableSets = mutableSetOf<Int>(6,10)
    // adding elements in the set
    mutableSets.add(4)
    mutableSets.add(5)
    for(item in mutableSets){
        println(item)
    }
}
```

Map   Because it is changeable, it can do operations such as put, remove, and clear. To show the mutable Map, write a Kotlin application.

```
fun main(args : Array<String>) {
    var mutableMaps = mutableMapOf<Int,String>(1 to
"Mahi",2 to "Nikita",3 to "Ruhi")
    // we can modify the element
    mutableMaps.put(1,"Praniti")
    // add one more element in the list
    mutableMaps.put(4,"Abhi")
    for(item in mutableMaps.values){
        println(item)
    }
}
```

ARRAYLIST IN KOTLIN

In Kotlin, the ArrayList class is used to generate a dynamic array. The term "dynamic array" refers to the ability to grow or reduce the size of an array based on the needs. It also has read and write capabilities. ArrayList is non-synchronized and may include duplicates. We use ArrayList to get the index of a specific member, convert an ArrayList to a string or another array, and for various other purposes.

Constructors:

1. **ArrayList<E>():** It creates an empty ArrayList.

2. **ArrayList(capacity: Int):** It creates an ArrayList of the specified size.

3. **ArrayList(elements: Collection<E>):** It create an ArrayList filled by collection elements.

Most Important Methods

add(index:Int, element: E): Boolean: It is used to add a specific element to the ArrayList. The second input includes the element to be added, which is required, and the first parameter is the index to which want to add element, which is optional and defaults to 1 + the last index of the array.

Example:

```
fun main(args: Array<String>) {
    // creation of an empty arraylist using
constructor
    var arraylists = ArrayList<String>()
    //adding String elements in the list
    arraylists.add("Peeks")
    arraylists.add("Peeks")
    // iterating the list
    println("Array list ---->")
    for(i in arraylists)
        println(c)
    arraylists.add( 1,  "of")
    println("Arraylists after insertion:")
    for(i in arraylists)
        println(c)
}
```

addAll(index: Int, elements: Collection): Boolean: It is used to add all elements of the provided collection at the specified index into the current list. The first parameter is the index value, which is also optional.

```
fun main(args: Array<String>) {
    // creating empty arraylist using constructor
```

```
    var arraylist=ArrayList<String>()
    //adding String elements in the list
    arraylists.add("Peeks")
    arraylists.add("of")
    arraylists.add("Peeks")
    // creating the new arraylist1
    var arraylists1=ArrayList<String>()
    //adding all elements from arraylists to arraylists1
    println("Elements in arraylist1:")
    arraylist1.addAll(arraylists)
    for(c in arraylists1)
        println(c)
}
```

get(index: Int): E: It is used to return the element in the list at the provided index.

```
fun main(args: Array<String>) {
    // creating thr empty arraylists using constructor
    var arraylists=ArrayList<Int>()
    // adding elements
    arraylists.add(20)
    arraylists.add(40)
    arraylists.add(90)
    arraylists.add(70)
    arraylists.add(60)

    // iterating through the elements
    for(c in arraylists)
    print("$c")
    println()
    println("Accessing the index 2 of arraylists:
"+arraylists.get(3))
}
```

set(index: Int, element: E):E: It is used to replace element at the given position in the current list with the elements passed as arguments.

```
fun main(args: Array<String>) {
    // creating the empty arraylist using constructor
    var arraylists=ArrayList<String>()
    // adding the elements
```

```
    arraylists.add("Peeks")
    arraylists.add("of")
    arraylists.add("Peeks:")
    arraylists.add("Portal")
    // iterating through elements
    for(i in arraylists)
        print("$c")
    println()
    // set element at index 3 with new string
    arraylist.set(3,"A computer Science portal for
students")
    // iterating through the elements
    for(i in arraylist)
        print("$c")
}
```

indexOf(element: E): Int: It is used to return the index of the first occurrence of the specified element in the list, or –1 if the specified element does not appear in the list.

```
fun main(args: Array<String>) {
    // creating empty arraylists using constructor
    var arraylists=ArrayList<String>()
    // adding the elements
    arraylists.add("Peeks")
    arraylists.add("of")
    arraylists.add("Peeks")

    // iterating through the elements
    for(c in arraylists)
        print("$c ")
    println()
    println("Index of the element is: "+arraylist
.indexOf("Peeks"))
}
```

remove(element: E): Boolean: If available, it is used to delete the first occurrence of the particular element from the current collection. Similarly for removing the element at index c we use removeAt(index).

```
fun main(args: Array<String>) {
    // creating empty arraylists using constructor
```

```
    var arraylists=ArrayList<String>()
    // adding the elements
    arraylists.add("Peeks")
    arraylists.add("for")
    arraylists.add("Peeks")
    arraylists.remove("of")
    // iterating through elements
    for(c in arraylists)
        print("$c ")
}
```

clear(): It is used to eliminate all of list's items.

```
fun main(args: Array<String>) {
    // creating empty arraylists using constructor
    var arraylists=ArrayList<Int>()
    // adding the elements
    arraylists.add(10)
    arraylists.add(20)
    arraylists.add(30)
    arraylists.add(40)
    arraylists.add(50)

    // iterating through the elements
    for(c in arraylist)
        print("$c")
    arraylist.clear()
    println()
    println("Size of arraylist after clearing all
elements: "+arraylists.size)
}
```

LISTOF() IN KOTLIN

A list is a collection of elements sorted in a specific way. Kotlin provides two types of lists: immutable (non-modifiable) and mutable (modifiable) (can be modified).

Read-only lists are produced using listOf(), and their items cannot edit, but mutable lists are generated with the mutableListOf() function and their elements may be altered or modified.

Integers are used in the Kotlin program list:

```kotlin
fun main(args: Array<String>) {
    val x = listOf('1', '2', '3')
    println(x.size)
    println(x.indexOf('2'))
    println(x[2])
}
```

Strings are used in a Kotlin program that has a list:

```kotlin
fun main(args: Array<String>) {
    //creating list of strings
    val x = listOf("Ramesh", "Shivay", "Rajat",
"Raqesh")
    println("The size of the list is: "+x.size)
    println("The index of the element Rajat is:
"+x.indexOf("Rajat"))
    println("The element at index "+x[2])
    for(i in x.indices){
        println(x[i])
    }
}
```

Indexing List Elements in Kotlin

Each list element has an index. The first entry has an index of zero (0), and the last element has an index of len − 1, where "len" is the list's length.

```kotlin
fun main(args: Array<String>)
{
    val numbs = listOf(11, 33, 27, 72, 0, 22, 21, 46, 10)
    val numb1 = numbs.get(0)
    println(numb1)
    val numb2 = numbs[7]
    println(numb2)
    val index1 = numbs.indexOf(1)
    println("first index of number is $index1")
    val index2 = numbs.lastIndexOf(1)
    println("last index of number is $index2")
    val index3 = numbs.lastIndex
    println("last index of the list is $index3")
}
```

The First and Last Elements

The first and last elements of the list may retrieve without utilizing the get() function.

```
fun main(args: Array<String>)
{
    val numbs = listOf(11, 55, 37, 31, 0, 23, 15, 46,
17)
    println(numbs.first())
    println(numbs.last())
}
```

Iteration Methods for Lists

This is the process of accessing the elements of a list one by one.

In Kotlin, there are various ways to accomplish this.

```
fun main(args: Array<String>)
{
    val names1 = listOf("Gopi", "Asim", "Shubhi",
"Aditi",
        "Dinesh", "Nikita", "Gautam")
    // method-1
    for (name in names1) {
        print("$name, ")
    }
    println()
    // method-2
    for (x in 0 until names1.size) {
        print("${names1[x]} ")
    }
    println()
    // method-3
    names.forEachIndexed({x, y -> println("names1[$x]
= $y")})
    // method 4
    val it: ListIterator<String> = names1.
listIterator()
    while (it.hasNext()) {
        val x = it.next()
        print("$x ")
    }
    println()
}
```

Explanation:

```
for (name in names1) {
    print ("$name, ")
}
```

The for loop iterates across the list. The variable "name" points to the next member in the list in each cycle.

```
for (x in 0 until names1.size) {
    print ("${names [x]} ")
}
```

This approach takes advantage of the list's size. The till keyword creates a range of list indexes.

```
names1.forEachIndexed({x, y -> println ("names1 [$x] =
$y")})
```

We loop over the list with index and value available in each iteration using the forEachIndexed() method.

```
val it: ListIterator = names1.listIterator()
    while (it.hasNext()) {
        val x = it.next()
        print ("$x ")
    }
```

Here we use a ListIterator to iterate through the list.

Sorting the List's Elements

The examples below demonstrate how to sort a list in ascending or descending order.

```
fun main(args: Array<String>)
{
    val lists = listOf (83, 24,17, 31,42, 33, 0, 55, 67 )
    val asc1 = lists.sorted()
    println (asc1)
    val desc1 = lists.sortedDescending()
    println (desc1)
}
```

Explanation:

```
val asc1 = list.sorted()
```

The list is sorted in the ascending order via the sorted() function.

```
val desc1 = lists.sortedDescending()
```

The list is sorted in descending order using the sortedDescending() function.

Contains() and ContainsAll() Functions

This method determines whether or not an element exists in the list.

```
fun main(args: Array<String>)
{
    val lists = listOf(8, 4, 7, 1, 2, 3, 0, 5, 6 )

    val res1 = lists.contains(0)
    if (res1)
        println("list contains 0")
    else
        println("list does not contain 0")
    val results = lists.containsAll(listOf(3, -1))
    if (results)
        println("list contains 3 and -1")
    else
        println("list does not contain 3 and -1")
}
```

Explanation:

```
val res = lists.contains(0)
```

Checks if the lists include 0 and return true or false (her true), saved in res1.

```
val result = list.containsAll(listOf(3, -1))
```

Checks whether the list contains the values 3 and −1.

SetOf () in Kotlin

The Kotlin Set interface is a general unordered collection of items that includes duplicates. Kotlin recognizes two kinds of sets: mutable and immutable.

```
setOf() is immutable, which implies it only provides
read-only functionality.
SetOf() is mutable, implying both read and write
functionality.
```

Syntax:

```
fun <D> setOf( vararg elements: D): Set<D>
```

Description: This method returns a new read-only set of the elements given.

The items are iterated over in the order in which they are stored.

setOf() function Kotlin program:

```kotlin
fun main(args: Array<String>)
{
    //declaring set of strings
    val seta1 = setOf("Peeks", "of", "Peeks")
    //declaring a set of characters
    val setb1 = setOf( "P", "o", "P" )
    //declaring set of integers
    val setc1 = setOf( 11, 12, 13, 14 )
    //traversing through set of strings
    for(item in seta1)
        print( item )
    println()
    //traversing through set of characters
    for(item in setb1)
        print( item )
    println()
    //traversing through set of integers
    for(item in setc1)
        print( "$item " )
}
```

Set Indexing

The index of the specified element can be obtained using the index functions indexOf() and lastIndexOf(). We may also use the elementAt() method to find elements at a given index.

Index-using Kotlin program:

```kotlin
fun main(args: Array<String>) {
    val captain = setOf("Kamal","Smridhi","Ruhi","Maya
nk","Ridhi","Daman")
    println("element at index 2 is: "+captain.
elementAt(2))
    println("index of element is: "+captain.
indexOf("Smridhi"))
    println("last index of element is: "+captain.
lastIndexOf("Ruhi"))
}
```

Set the first() and last() element: The first() and last() methods may be used to obtain the first and last element of a set.

Example:

```kotlin
fun main(args: Array<String>){
    val captain = setOf(1,2,3,4,"Kanika",
"Smridhi",
        "Ruhi","Mayank","Ridhi","Daman")

    println("first element of the set is:
"+captain.first())
    println("last element of the set is:
"+captain.last())
}
```

Set Basics

We will go over fundamental methods such as count(), max(), min(), sum(), and average().

Basic functions are used in a Kotlin program:

```kotlin
fun main(args: Array<String>) {
    val nums = setOf(11, 22, 33, 44, 55, 66, 77, 88)
    println("number of element in the set is:
"+nums.count())
```

```
    println("maximum element in the set is: "+nums.
max())
    println("minimum element in the set is: "+nums.
min())
    println("sum of the elements in the set is:
"+nums.sum())
    println("average of elements in the set is:
"+nums.average())
}
```

Contains() and ContainsAll() Functions

Both approaches are used to determine whether or not an element exists in the set.

Kotlin program that use the contains() and containsAll() functions:

```
fun main(args: Array<String>){
    val captain = setOf(1,2,3,4,"Kanika","Smridhi",
        "Ruhi","Mayank","Ridhi","Daman")
    var names = "Daman"
    println("set contains the element $name or not?" +
            "    "+captain.contains(names))
    var nums = 5
    println("set contains the element $nums or not?" +
            "    "+captain.contains(nums))
    println("set contains the given elements or not?" +
            "    "+captain.containsAll(setOf(1,3,
"Ruhi")))
}
```

Checking the equality of empty sets and employing the isEmpty() functions:

```
fun <D> setOf(): Set <D>
```

This syntax returns an empty set of the specified type.

Kotlin program that use the isEmpty() function:

```
fun main(args: Array<String>) {
    //creation of an empty set of strings
    val seta1 = setOf<String>()
    //creation of an empty set of integers
    val setb1 =setOf<Int>()
```

```
    //the checking if set is empty or not
    println("seta1.isEmpty() is ${seta1.isEmpty()}")
    // Since the Empty sets are equal
    //checking if the two sets are equal or not
    println("seta1 == setb1 is ${seta1 == setb1}")
    println(seta1) //printing first set
}
```

MUTABLESETOF() METHOD IN KOTLIN

The Kotlin Set interface is a general unordered collection of elements that includes duplicates. Kotlin recognizes two kinds of sets: changeable and immutable.

SetOf() is immutable, which implies it only provides read-only functionality.

SetOf() is mutable, implying both read and write operations.

Syntax:

```
fun <D> mutableSetOf( vararg elements: D): MutableSet
<D>
```

Description:

- This method returns a collection of provided items that can be read and written.

- The iteration order of the elements is preserved in the returned set.

The following Kotlin code implements the mutableSetOf() function:

```
fun main(args: Array<String>)
{
    //declaring mutable set of integers
    val mutableSetA1 = mutableSetOf<Int>( 11,   22,
33,   44,   33);
    println(mutableSetA1)
    //declaring mutable set of strings
    val mutableSetB1 = mutableSetOf<String>("Peeks","o
f",   "Peeks");
    println(mutableSetB1)
    //declaring empty mutable set of integers
```

```
    val mutableSetC1 = mutableSetOf<Int>()
    println(mutableSetC1)
}
```

Adding and Deleting Elements from a Set

We may use the add() method to add elements to a mutable set, and the remove () function to remove elements.

Example:

```
fun main(args: Array<String>)
{
    //declaring mutable set of integers
    val seta1 = mutableSetOf( 11,  22,  33,
44,  33);
    println(seta1);
    //adding the elements 66 & 77
    seta1.add(66);
    seta1.add(77);
    println(seta1);
    //removing the 33 from the set
    seta1.remove(33);
    println(seta1);
    //another way to add the elements is by using
listOf() function
    seta1 += listOf(88,99)
    println(seta1)
}
```

Set Indexing

The index of the specified element may be obtained using the index methods indexOf() and lastIndexOf(). We may also use the elementAt() method to find elements at a given index.

Index-using Kotlin program:

```
fun main(args: Array<String>) {
    val captain = mutableSetOf("Kanika","Smridhi",
"Ruhi","Mayank","Ridhi","Daman")
    println("The element at index 2 is: "+captain.
elementAt(2))
```

```
    println("The index of element is: "+captain.
indexOf("Smridhi"))
    println("The last index of element is: "+captain.
lastIndexOf("Ridhi"))
}
```

Set the First and Last Element

The first() and last() methods may use to obtain the first and last element of a set.

Example:

```
fun main(args: Array<String>){
    val captain = mutableSetOf(11,22,33,44,"Kanika
","Smridhi",
        "Ruhi","Mayank","Daman","Ridhi")
    println("first element of the set is:
"+captain.first())
    println("last element of the set is:
"+captain.last())
}
```

Traversal in a MutableSet

In a MutableSet, we can perform for loop using an iterator to traverse all the elements in the set.

```
fun main(args: Array<String>)
{
    //declaring a mutable set of integers
    val seta1 = mutableSetOf( 11,  22,  33,  44,  33);
    //traversal of the seta1 using an iterator 'item'
    for(item in seta1)
        println( item )
}
```

Contains() and ContainsAll() Methods

Both approaches are used to determine whether or not an element exists in the set.

Kotlin program that use the contains() and containsAll() functions:

```
fun main(args: Array<String>){
    val captain = mutableSetOf(11,22,33,44,"Kanika","S
mridhi",
        "Ruhi","Mayank","Ridhi","Daman")
    var names = "Daman"
    println("set contains the element $names or not?" +
        "   "+captain.contains(names))
    var nums = 5
    println("set contains the element $nums or not?" +
        "   "+captain.contains(nums))
    println("set contains the given elements or not?" +
        "   "+captain.containsAll(setOf(1,3,
"Root")))
}
```

Checking the equality of empty sets and employing the isEmpty() functions:

```
fun <D> mutableSetOf(): mutableSet <D>
```

This syntax returns an empty set of the specified type.
Kotlin program that use the isEmpty() function:

```
fun main(args: Array<String>) {
    //creating empty set of strings
    val seta1 = mutableSetOf<String>()
    //creating empty set of integers
    val setb1 = mutableSetOf<Int>()


    //checking if the set is empty or not
    println("seta1.isEmpty() is ${seta1.isEmpty()}")
    // Since empty sets are equal
    //checking if the two sets are equal or not
    println("seta1 == setb1 is ${seta1 == setb1}")
    println(seta1) //printing first set
}
```

HASHSETOF() IN KOTLIN

Kotlin HashSet is a generic unordered collection of elements that contains no duplicates. It is responsible for implementing the set interface. hashSetOf() is a function that returns a mutable HashSet that may be read as well as written. The HashSet class uses hashing to store all of the elements.

Syntax:

```
fun <D> hashSetOf(vararg elements: T): HashSet <D>
```

It returns a new HashSet containing the requested elements but makes no guarantees regarding the order sequence indicated at the time of storing.

Example:

```
fun main(args: Array<String>)
{
    //declaring hash set of integers
    val seta1 = hashSetOf(11,22,33,33);
    //printing the first set
    println(seta1)
    //declaring hash set of strings
    val setb1 = hashSetOf("Peeks","of","peeks");
    println(setb1);
}
```

Adding and Deleting Elements from a HashSet

- The add() and addAll() methods can use to add elements to a HashSet.

- Using the remove() method, we may delete an element.

Program of using the add() and remove() method:

```
fun main(args: Array<String>)
{
    //declaring a hash set of integers
    val seta1 = hashSetOf<Int>();
    println(seta1)
    //adding elements
    seta1.add(11)
    seta1.add(22)
```

```
    //making extra set to add it in seta
    val newsets = setOf(44,55,66)
    seta1.addAll(newsets)
    println(seta1)
    //removing 22 from the set
    seta1.remove(22)
    println(seta1)
}
```

HashSet Traversal

We can traverse HashSet using an iterator in a loop.

```
fun main(args: Array<String>)
{
    //declaring hash set of integers
    val seta1 = hashSetOf(11,22,33,55);
    //traversing in set using a for loop
    for(items in seta1)
        println(items)
}
```

Indexing in a HashSet

Using the index methods indexOf() and lastIndexOf(), we may get the index of the specified element. We may also use the elementAt() method to find elements at a given index.

Index-using Kotlin program:

```
fun main(args: Array<String>) {
    val captain = hashSetOf("Kanika","Sumit","Ruhi","M
ayank","Ridhi","Daman")
    println("element at index 2 is: "+captain.
elementAt(3))
    println("index of element is: "+captain.
indexOf("Smridhi"))
    println("last index of element is: "+captain.
lastIndexOf("Ridhi"))
}
```

Contains() and ContainsAll() Functions

Both methods are used to determine whether or not an element exists in the HashSet.

Kotlin program that use the contains() and containsAll() functions:

```
fun main(args: Array<String>){
    val captain = hashSetOf(1,2,3,4,"Kanika","Smridhi",
        "Ruhi","Mayank","Ridhi","Daman")
    var names = "Ridhi"
    println("set contains the element $name or not?" +
        "    "+captain.contains(names))
    var nums = 5
    println("set contains the element $nums or not?" +
        "    "+captain.contains(nums))
    println("set contains the given elements or not?" +
        "    "+captain.containsAll(setOf(11,33,"Dam
an","Waner")))
}
```

Checking the equality of empty hash sets and employing the isEmpty() functions:

```
fun <D> hashSetOf(): hashSet <D>
```

This syntax returns an empty hash set of a given type.

Kotlin program that use the isEmpty() function:

```
fun main(args: Array<String>) {
    //creating empty hash set of strings
    val seta1 = hashSetOf<String>()
    //creating empty hashset of integers
    val setb1 =hashSetOf<Int>()
    //checking if the set is empty or not
    println("seta1.isEmpty() is ${seta1.isEmpty()}")
    // Since Empty hashsets are equal
    //checking if the two hash sets are equal or not
    println("seta1 == setb1 is ${seta1 == setb1}")
}
```

MAPOF() in Kotlin

A Kotlin Map is a collection of pairings of objects. The data in a Map is stored in the form of pairs, each of which consists of a key and a value. Map keys are one-of-a-kind, and the Map only stores one value for each key.

Kotlin makes a distinction between immutable and mutable Maps. Immutable Maps generated with mapOf() are read-only, but mutable Maps made with mutableMapOf() may be read and written.

Syntax:

```
fun <X, Y> mapOf(vararg pairs: Pair<X, Y>): Map<X, Y>
```

- The pair's first value is the key, and the second is the value of the associated key.

- If many pairs have the same key, the Map will return the last pair's value.

- The Map entries are traversed in the order indicated.

mapOf() Kotlin program:

```
fun main(args: Array<String>)
{
    //declaring map of integer to string
    val map1 = mapOf(1 to "Peeks", 2 to "of",
3 to "Peeks")
    //printing map
    println( map1)
}
```

Map keys, values, and entries:

```
fun main(args: Array<String>)
{
    //declaring map of integer to string
    val map1 = mapOf(1 to "One", 2 to "Two",  3 to
"Three", 4 to "Four")
    println("Map Entries : "+map1)
    println("Map Keys: "+map1.keys )
    println("Map Values: "+map1.values )
}
```

Map Size

There are two ways to determine the size of a Map. By using the Map's size property and the count() method.

```kotlin
fun main() {
    val ranks1 = mapOf(1 to "London",2 to "Africa",3
to "Germany",4 to "Canada")
    //method 1
    println("size of the map is: "+ranks1.size)
    //method 2
    println("size of the map is: "+ranks1.count())
}
```

Empty Map

Using mapOf, we may generate an empty serializable map ().

MapOf() Example:

```kotlin
fun main(args: Array<String>)
{
    //created an empty map using mapOf()
    val map = mapOf<String,  Int>()
    println("Entries: " + map.entries)   //entries of
the map
    println("Keys:" + map.keys)   //keys of the map
    println("Values:" + map.values)   //values of the map
}
```

Get Map Values

We may retrieve values from a Map using the various ways outlined in the following program:

```kotlin
fun main() {
    val ranks1 = mapOf(1 to "London",2 to "Africa",3
to "Germany",4 to "Canada")
    //method 1
    println("The Team having rank #1 is: "+ranks1[1])
    //method 2
    println("The Team having rank #3 is: "+ranks1.
getValue(3))
    //method 3
    println("The Team having rank #4 is: "+ranks1.
getOrDefault(4, 0))
    // method  4
    val teams = ranks1.getOrElse(2, { 0 })
    println(teams)
}
```

Map Contains Keys or Values

Using the containsKey() and containsValue() methods, we can detect if a Map contains a key or a value.

```kotlin
fun main() {
    val colorsTopToBottom = mapOf("green" to 1,
"yellow" to 2, "pink" to 3,
        "white" to 4, "brown" to 5, "blue" to 6,
"purple" to 7)
    var colors = "yellow"
    if (colorsTopToBottom.containsKey(colors)) {
        println("Yes, it contains the color
$colors")
    } else {
        println("No, it does not contain the color
$colors")
    }
    val values = 8
    if (colorsTopToBottom.containsValue(values)) {
        println("Yes, it contains the value
$values")
    } else {
        println("No, it does not contain the value
$values")
    }
}
```

Two Values and the Same Key

If two values have the same key value, the Map will include the latest value of those numbers.

Example:

```kotlin
fun main(args: Array<String>)
{
    //lets make the two values with same key
    val map1 = mapOf(1 to "peeks1",2 to "of",  1
to "peeks2")
    // return map entries
    println("Entries of map: " + map1.entries)
}
```

Explanation: In this case, key value 1 has been set with two values: peeks1 and peeks2, but because mapOf() may only have one value for one key item, the Map only stores the last value, and peeks1 is removed.

HASHMAP IN KOTLIN

Kotlin HashMap is a collection that includes object pairs. MutableMap implementation in Kotlin using Hash Tables. It keeps data in the form of a key and value pair. Map keys are one-of-a-kind, and the Map only stores one value for each key. It's represented as HashMapkey, value> or HashMapK, V>.

HashMap's hash table-based implementation makes no guarantees regarding the order of given data of key, value, and collection elements.

Kotlin HashMap class constructors are available: Kotlin HashMap has four constructors, each with a public access modifier:

- **HashMap():** The default constructs that create an empty HashMap object.

- **HashMap(initialCapacity: Int, loadFactor: Float = 0f):** This function is used to create a HashMap with the provided capacity. If initialCapacity and loadFactor are not utilized, they will disregard.

- **HashMap(initialCapacity: Int):** This method creates a HashMap with the supplied capacity. If initialCapacity is not utilized, it will be disregarded.

- **HashMap(original: Map <out K, V>):** This method generates a HashMap instance with the same mappings as the supplied Map.

Uses of HashMap functions: Kotlin program that uses the functions HashMap(), HashMap(original: Map), Traversing HashMap, and HashMap.get():

```
fun main(args: Array<String>) {
    //example of HashMap class define
    // with the empty "HashMap of <String, Int>"
    var hashMap1 : HashMap<String, Int>
            = HashMap<String, Int> ()
    //printing empty hashMap
    printHashMap(hashMap1)
    //adding elements to the hashMap1 using
    // put() function
```

```
    hashMap1.put("IronMan",  3200)
    hashMap1.put("Thor",  100)
    hashMap1.put("SpiderMan",  1300)
    hashMap1.put("NickFury",  1100)
    hashMap1.put("HawkEye",  1400)
    //printing the non-Empty hashMap1
    printHashMap(hashMap1)
    //using overloaded print function of
    //Kotlin language to get same results
    println("hashMap1 : " + hashMap1 + "\n")

    //hashMap1 traversal using a for loop
    for(key in hashMap1.keys){
        println("Element at key $key :
${hashMap1[key]}")
    }
    //creating another hashMap1 object with
    // the previous version of hashMap1 object
    var secondHashMap : HashMap<String, Int>
            = HashMap<String, Int> (hashMap1)
    println("\n" + "Second HashMap : ")
    for(key in secondHashMap.keys){
        //using hashMap1.get() function to fetch the
values
        println("The Element at key $key : ${hashMap1.
get(key)}")
    }
    //this will clear whole map and make it empty
    println("hashMap1.clear()")
    hashMap1.clear()
    println("After Clearing : " + hashMap1)
}
//function to print hashMap1
fun printHashMap(hashMap1: HashMap<String, Int>){
    // isEmpty() function to check whether
    // the hashMap1 is empty or not
    if(hashMap1.isEmpty()){
        println("hashMap1 is empty")
    }else{
        println("hashMap1: " + hashMap1)
    }
}
```

HashMap initial capacity, HashMap.size – Kotlin program:

```kotlin
fun main(args: Array<String>) {
    //HashMap can also be initializing
    // with initial capacity.
    //The capacity can be changed by
    // adding and replacing element.
    var hashMap1 : HashMap<String, Int>
            = HashMap<String, Int> (4)

    //adding elements to the hashMap1 using put()
function
    hashMap1.put("Iron-Man", 3300)
    hashMap1.put("Thor", 200)
    hashMap1.put("Spider-Man", 1500)
    hashMap1.put("Nick-Fury", 1300)

    for(key in hashMap1.keys) {
        println("Element at key $key :
${hashMap1[key]}")
    }
    //return the size of hashMap1
    println("\n" + "hashMap1.size : " + hashMap1.size )

    //adding a new element in the hashMap
    hashMap1["Black-Widow"] = 3300;
    println("hashMap1.size : " + hashMap1.size + "\n")

    for(key in hashMap1.keys) {
        println("Element at key $key :
${hashMap1[key]}")
    }
}
```

Kotlin program that employs the HashMap.get(key), HashMap. replace(), and HashMap.put() functionalities:

```kotlin
fun main(args: Array<String>) {
    var hashMap1 : HashMap<String, Int>
            = HashMap<String, Int> ()
    //adding elements to the hashMap1
    // using put() function
```

```
hashMap1.put("Iron-Man", 3200)
hashMap1.put("Thor", 120)
hashMap1.put("Spider-Man", 1300)
hashMap1.put("Cap", 1400)
for(key in hashMap1.keys) {
    println("Element at the key $key :
${hashMap1[key]}")
}
//the hashMap1's elements can be accessed like
this
println("\nhashMap1[\"Iron-Man\"] : "
        + hashMap1["Iron-Man"])
hashMap1["Thor"] = 2000
println("hashMap1.get(\"Thor\") : "
        + hashMap1.get("Thor") + "\n")
//replacing some value
hashMap1.replace("Cap", 989);
hashMap1.put("Thor", 2200);
println("hashMap1.replace(\"Cap\", 989)" +
        " hashMap1.replace(\"Thor\", 2200)) :")
for(key in hashMap1.keys) {
    println("Element at key $key : ${hashMap1
[key]}")
}
}
```

HashMap Time Complexity

If the hash function is designed correctly and the items are appropriately dispersed, Kotlin HashMap gives constant time or O(1) complexity for fundamental operations like get and put. When searching in a HashMap, containsKey() is merely a get() that throws away the received result; therefore, it's O(1) (assuming the hash function works properly).

Other features of the Kotlin HashMap class include:

- **Boolean consistsKey(key: K):** This function returns true if the Map consists of the specified key.

- **Boolean containsValue(value: V):** If the Map maps one or more keys to the supplied value, it returns true.

- **void clear():** It eliminates all Map elements.

- **remove(key: K):** It deletes the provided key and associated value from the Map.

ANNOTATIONS IN KOTLIN

Annotations are a Kotlin feature that allows the programmer to embed additional information in the source file. This information, however, does not affect the program's activities. A variety of tools utilizes this data during both development and deployment.

The following arguments are typically included in annotations and must be compile-time constants:

- Primitive types (Int, Long etc.)

- Strings

- Enumerations

- Class

- Other annotations

- Arrays of the types mentioned above

Using Annotation

We may use annotation by placing its name in front of a code element and prefixing it with the @ symbol. For example, if we want to use the annotation Positive, we should write the following. If we want to use the annotation Pos, we should write the following:

```
@Positive val x: Int
```

Similar to a function call, an argument can be passed to an annotation in parentheses.

```
@Allowedlanguage("Kotlin")
```

The @ symbol should be omitted when an annotation is used as a parameter in another annotation, the @ symbol should be omitted. We've used the Replacewith() annotation as a parameter here.

```
@Deprecated("function is deprecated, use = = =
instead", ReplaceWith("this = = = other"))
```

When an annotation parameter is a class object, we should add::class to the class name as:

```
@Throws(IOException::class)
```

Declaring Annotation

An annotation is declared by prefixing the class keyword with the annotation keyword. Annotation declarations, by definition, cannot include code. When we declare our annotations, we must describe which code components they may apply to and where they should be kept.

The most basic annotation has no parameters:

```
annotation class Myexample
```

Annotation with a parameter is similar to a class with a main constructor:

```
annotation class Suffix(val s1: String)
```

Annotate a Constructor

We may also annotate the constructor of a class. It is possible to accomplish this by utilizing the constructor keyword for constructor declaration and inserting the annotation before it.

```
class Myexample@Inject constructor(dependency:
MyDependency) {
//....
}
```

Annotate a Property

We may annotate the class's properties by adding annotations to the properties. We assume that a Lang instance is valid if the name value is either Kotlin or Java in the following example.

```
class Lang (
    @Allowedlanguages(["Java","Kotlin"]) val name:
String)
}
```

Several Built-in Annotations

Kotlin has some built-in annotations that may provide extra attributes to user-defined annotations. These annotations, to be more specific, are used to annotate annotations.

@Target

This annotation indicates where the annotated annotation can be used, such as classes, functions, constructors, type parameters, and so on. The constructor's keyword comes before the constructors when an annotation is given to a class's primary constructors.

To explain the @Target annotation, consider the following example:

```
@Target(AnnotationTarget.CONSTRUCTOR,
AnnotationTarget.LOCAL_VARIABLE)
annotation class AnnotationDemo2
class XYZ @AnnotationDemo2 constructor(val count:Int){
    fun display(){
        println("Constructor-annotated")
        println("Count is $count")
    }
}
fun main(){
    val obj =  XYZ(5)
    obj.display()
    @AnnotationDemo2 val message: String
    message = "Hellooo"
    println("Local-parameter-annotated")
    println(message)
}
```

@Retention

This annotation indicates the availability of the annotated annotation, i.e., whether it remains in the source file or is available at runtime, and so on. Its mandatory argument must be an instance of the AnnotationRetention enumeration with the following elements:

- SOURCE

- BINARY

- RUNTIME

To explain the @Retention annotation, consider the following example:

```
//Specifying annotation with the runtime policy
@Retention(AnnotationRetention.RUNTIME)
annotation class AnnotationDemo3
@AnnotationDemo3 fun main(){
    println("Main-function-annotated")
}
```

@Repeatable

This annotation allows an element to have applied the same annotation numerous times. This annotation can only use with the Retention Policy set to SOURCE in the present version of Kotlin 1.3.

Example:

```
@Repeatable
@Retention(AnnotationRetention.SOURCE)
annotation class AnnotationDemo4 (val value: Int)
@AnnotationDemo4(4)
@AnnotationDemo4(5)
fun main(){
     println("The Repeatable Annotation applied on
main")
}
```

REFLECTION IN KOTLIN

Reflection is a set of the language and library capabilities that enable runtime introspection of a particular program. Kotlin reflection is used at runtime to access a class and its members, such as properties, functions, constructors, etc.

Along with the Java reflection API, Kotlin has its own set of reflection API, which is written in a simple, functional manner. The standard Java Reflection constructs are likewise accessible in Kotlin and are fully compatible with its code.

Kotlin reflections are accessible in the following languages:

`kotlin.reflect package`

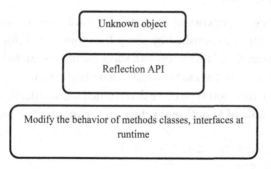

Reflection of Kotlin.

Kotlin reflection characteristics:

- Kotlin reflection provides access to properties and nullable types.

- Kotlin reflection differs from Java reflection in a few ways.

- Kotlin reflection facilitates access to JVM code created by a language.

Class References

Use the class reference operator to acquire a statically known class reference at runtime. In addition, a reference to a class can be derived from its instances; such references are known as bounded class references. In the case of inheritance, you may gain a reference to the specific type to which the object adheres by using instances.

As an example of class references, consider the following:

```kotlin
//sample empty class
class DemoReflection {
}
fun main()
{
    // Reference obtained using classname
    val xyz = DemoReflection::class
    println("This is a class reference $xyz")
    // the reference obtained using object
    val obj = DemoReflection()
    println("This is bounded class reference
${obj::class}")
}
```

Function References

We may retrieve a functional reference for each named function defined in Kotlin. This is accomplished by using the :: operator before the function name. These functional references can subsequently be passed to other functions as arguments. In the case of overloaded functions, we may either explicitly provide the function type or be determined automatically from the text.

As an example of functional references, consider the following:

```kotlin
fun add(x: Int,y: Int) : Int{
    return x+y;
}
```

```
fun add(x: String,y: String): String{
    return """$x$y"""
}

fun isDivisibleBy3(x: Int): Boolean{
    return x%3 == 0
}
fun main(){
    // the function reference obtained using ::
operator
    val ref1 = ::isDivisibleBy3
    val array = listOf<Int>(11,2,34,46,5,64,7,82,91)
    println(array.filter(ref1))
    // The function reference obtained for an
overloaded function
    // By explicitly specifying type
    val ref2: (String,String) -> String = ::add;
    println(ref2)
    // Function reference obtained implicitly
    val c = add(13,2)
    println(c)
}
```

Property References

We can get property references in the same way we get function references by using the :: operator. If the property is part of a class, the classname must also be given using the :: operator. These property references enable us to treat a property as an object, retrieving its values using the get method and editing it using the set function.

As an example of a property reference, consider the following:

```
class Example(var x: Float){
}
val a = 10;
fun main(){
    // Property Reference for package level property
    val b = ::a
    println(b.get())
    println(b.name)

    // Property Reference for class property
    val c = Property::x
    println(c.get(Property(5.899f)))
}
```

Constructor References

A class's constructor references can access the same way as method and property references. These references can use to point to a function that returns an object of the same type. These applications, however, are uncommon.

As an example of constructor references, consider the following:

```
class Example(var x: Float){
}
fun main(){
    // The Constructor Reference
    val a = ::Property
    println(a.name)
}
```

OVERLOADING OF THE KOTLIN OPERATOR

Because Kotlin supports user-defined types, it also can overload standard operators, making it easier to deal with user-defined types. Overloading is possible for all unary, binary, and relational operators. The operators are overloaded using either member functions or extension functions. The operator modifier comes before these functions. Every operator has standard functions that can be overloaded based on use.

Unary Operators

The following table shows the different functions that can define for unary operators. These functions make changes to the caller instance.

Operator Expression	Corresponding Function
+y	y.unaryPlus()
−y	y.unaryMinus()
!y	y.not()

In this case, y represents the type for which the operator is defined. The overloaded functionality is defined inside the functions themselves.

The following Kotlin program demonstrates unary operator overloading:

```
class OverloadUnary (var str:String) {
    // overloading function
    operator fun unaryMinus() {
```

```
        str1 = str1.reversed()
    }
}
// the main function
fun main(args : Array<String>) {
    val obj1 = OverloadUnary ("HELLOOO")
    println("Initial string is ${obj1.str}")y
    //calling overloaded function unaryMinus()
    -obj1
    println("String after applying unary operator
${obj1.str1}")
}
```

Increment and Decrement Operators

The increment and decrement operators for type can be defined using the following functions. These functions return a new instance with the result of the expression.

Operator Expression	Corresponding Function
++y	y.inc()
--y	y.dec()

When used in either postfix or prefix notation, these functions perform well in both cases, producing the same expected output.

Program using Kotlin to show operator overloading:

```
class OverloadIncDec(var str:String) {
    // overloading the increment function
    operator fun inc():OverloadIncDec {
        val obj1 = IncDecOverload(this.str)
        obj.str1 = obj1.str1 + 'a'
        return obj1
    }
    // overloading the decrement function
    operator fun dec(): IncDecOverload {
        val obj1 = IncDecOverload(this.str)
        obj.str1 = obj1.str1.substring(0,obj1.str1.
length-1)
        return obj1
    }
    override fun toString(): String {
```

```
        return str1
    }
}
// the main function
fun main(args: Array<String>) {
    var obj1 = OverloadIncDec("Helloo")
    println(obj1++)
    println(obj1--)
    println(++obj1)
    println(--obj1)
}
```

Binary Operators

The following table lists the binary operators and their equivalent functions. All of these functions have an effect on the calling instance.

Operator Expression	Corresponding Function
y1 + y2	y1.plus(y2)
y1 – y2	y1.minus(y2)
y1 * y2	y1.times(y2)
y1/ y2	y1.div(y2)
y1% y2	y1.rem(y2)
y1..y2	y1.rangeTo(y2)

Program to overload the plus function:

```
class Objects(var objName: String) {
    // Overloading function
    operator fun plus(x: Int) {
        objNames = "Name is $objNames and data is $x"
    }
    override fun toString(): String {
        return objNames
    }
}
//the main function
fun main() {
    val obj1 = Objects("Chairs")
    // Calling overloaded function
    obj1+9
    println(obj1)
}
```

Note that the relational operators have no specified functions; nevertheless, the type must implement the comparable interface to utilize relational operators on instances of a user-defined type.

Other Operators

Because Kotlin provides a diverse set of operators, specifying each for a type is not a good programming practice. The following table lists some of the additional useful operators in Kotlin that may be overloaded.

Operator Expression	Corresponding Function
y1 in y2	y2.contains(y1)
y1 !in y2	!y2.contains(y1)
y[i]	y.get(i)
y[i, j]	y.get(i, j)
y[i] = b	y.set(i, b)
y[i, j] = b	y.set(i, j, b)
y()	y.invoke()
y(i)	y.invoke(i)
y(i, j)	y.invoke(i, j)
y1 += y2	y1.plusAssign(y2)
y1 −= y2	y1.minusAssign(y2)
y1 *= y2	y1.timesAssign(y2)
y1 /= y2	y1.divAssign(y2)
y1 %= y2	y1.remAssign(y2)

KOTLIN DESTRUCTURING DECLARATIONS

In the form of destructuring declarations, Kotlin gives the programmer a one-of-a-kind technique to interact with class instances. A destructuring declaration generates and initializes many variables at the same time.

Example:

```
val (emps_id,salary) = employees
```

These several variables relate to a class's attributes connected with an instance. We may utilize these variables separately in any way we choose.

```
println(emps_id+" "+salary)
```

The destructing declaration is based on the component() function notion. The class provides the number of component functions that correspond to the number of variables that a destructing declaration can declare, beginning with component1(), component2(), and continuing up to componentN(). In Kotlin, the data class is used by default to implement component functions.

The following code was generated from the destructuring declaration:

```
val emps_id = employees.component1()
val salary = employees.component2()
```

Program of returning the two values from a function:

```
data class Datas(val name:String,val age:Int)
// A function returning two values
fun sendData():Datas{
    return Datas("Jackie",32)
}

fun main(){
    val obj1 = sendData()
    // Using instance to access the properties
    println("Name is ${obj1.name}")
    println("Age is ${obj1.age}")

    // Creating two variables using the destructing
declaration
    val (names,ages) = sendData()
    println("Name is $names")
    println("Age is $ages")
}
```

If used in a destructuring declaration, the component function definitions must be preceded by the operator keyword.

Underscore for unneeded variables: We may wish to disregard a variable in a destructuring declaration at times. To do so, substitute an underscore for its name. The component function for the provided variable is not called in this scenario.

Destructuring Declaration in Lambdas

As of Kotlin 1.1, the destructing declaration syntax may also use for lambda arguments. If a lambda argument has a Pair or another type that defines component functions, we can add extra parameters by placing them in parentheses. The regulations are the same as they were previously specified.

Program with lambda arguments that use destructuring declaration:

```
fun main(){
    val map = mutableMapOf<Int,String>()
    map.put(1,"Ishaan")
    map.put(2,"Kamini")
    map.put(3,"Kasika")
    map.put(4,"Minalv")
    map.put(5,"Nita")
    map.put(6,"Pratyushi")
    map.put(7,"Shama")
    map.put(8,"Subhash")
    map.put(9,"Udit")
    map.put(10,"Vidhi")
    println("The Initial map is")
    println(map)
    // Destructuring a map entry into key and values
    val newmap = map.mapValues { (key,value) -> "Hello ${value}" }
    println("Map after appending the Hello")
    println(newmap)
}
```

EQUALITY EVALUATION

Kotlin includes comparing instances of a specific type in two separate ways. This characteristic distinguishes Kotlin from other programming languages.

There are two sorts of equality:

- Structural Equality
- Referential Equality

Structural Equality

Structural equality is tested using the == operator and its opposite, the != operator. By default, the phrase x==y is converted into a call to the type's equals() method.

```
x?.equals(y)? : (y = = = null)
```

Specifies that if x is not equal to null, the function equals(y) is called; otherwise, if x is determined to be null, it tries to see whether y is referentially equal to null.

Note: When (x = = null), it is immediately translated to referential equality (x = = = null); therefore, no code optimization is required.

As a result, to use = = on instances of a type, the type must override the equals() method.

The structural equality of a string compares its contents.

Referential Equality

In Kotlin, referential equality is tested using the === operator and its opposite, the !== operator. This equality returns true only if two instances of the same type refer to the same memory address. When used on types that are transformed to primitives at runtime, the === check is converted to == check, and the !== check is converted to != check.

Program using Kotlin to illustrate structural and referential equality:

```kotlin
class Squares(val side: Int) {
    override fun equals(other: Any?): Boolean {
        if(other is Squares){
            return other.side == side
        }
        return false
    }
}
//the main function
fun main(args :Array<String>) {
    val squares1 = Square(4)
    val squares2 = Square(7)
    // structural equality
    if(squares1 == squares2) {
        println("The Two squares are structurally
equal")
    }
    // the referential equality
    if(squares1 !== squares2) {
        println("The Two squares are not referentially
equal")
    }
}
```

KOTLIN COMPARATOR

When a new type is required in a programming context, the problem of arranging the instances of that type becomes a crucial one. We implement the comparable interface to compare two instances of a type. However, since they must be compared automatically in ordering instances, and because the order might vary depending on numerous criteria, Kotlin offers a basic comparator interface. This interface compares and organizes two items of the same type.

Function

compare: This function compares two instances of the same type and returns zero if they are equal, a negative integer if the second instance is larger, and a positive number otherwise.

```
abstract fun compare(x: T, y: T): Int
```

Functions of Extension

reversed: This function accepts a comparator as an input and returns the comparator with the same ordering as the passed comparator.

```
fun <D> Comparator<D>. reversed(): Comparator<D>
```

then: This function combines two comparator, and the second one is utilized only when the values in the first comparator are equal.

```
infix fun <D> Comparator<D>.
then(
    comparator: Comparator<in D>
): Comparator<D>
```

As an example, consider the compare, then, and reversed functions:

```
class Names(val firstNames: String,val lastNames:
String){
    override fun toString(): String {
        return """$firstNames $lastNames"""
    }
}
```

```kotlin
// comparator to compare the first names of Names
class ComparatorOne: Comparator<Names>{
    override fun compare(o1: Names?, o2: Names?): Int
{
        if(o1 == null || o2 == null){
            return 0;
        }
        return o1.firstNames.compareTo(o2.firstNames)
    }
}

// comparator to compare last names of Names
class AnotherComparator: Comparator<Names>{
    override fun compare(o1: Name?, o2: Name?): Int {
        if(o1 == null || o2 == null)
            return 0
        return o1.lastNames.compareTo(o2.lastNames)
    }
}

fun main(){
    val lists = ArrayList<Name>()
    lists.add(Names("Stev","Wau"))
    lists.add(Names("Stev","Smiti"))
    lists.add(Names("Virati","Sohli"))
    lists.add(Names("Kani","Will"))
    lists.add(Names("Joti","Ruhan"))

    println("The lists is:")
    println(lists)

    val comparatorOne = ComparatorOne()
    // Sorting the list according to first names
    lists.sortWith(comparatorOne)
    println("The List sorted according to first name")
    println(lists)

    val anotherComparator = AnotherComparator()
    val finalComparator = comparatorOne.
then(anotherComparator)
    // Sorting the list according to first name then
by last name
    list.sortWith(finalComparator)
```

```
    println("The List sorted according to first name
and last name")
    println(lists)

    val reverseComparator = finalComparator.reversed()
    // Reverse sorting the lists
    lists.sortWith(reverseComparator)
    println("Lists reverse sorted")
    println(lists)
}
```

thenBy: This function converts the type instances to comparable instances and then compares them with these instances.

```
fun <D> Comparator<D>.thenBy(
    selector: (D) -> Comparable<*>?
): Comparator<D>
```

thenByDescending: This method returns a descending comparator that transforms a value into a comparable instance before comparing the instances.

```
inline fun <D> Comparator<D>.
thenByDescending(
    crossinline selector: (D) -> Comparable<*>?
): Comparator<D>
```

Example to describe the thenBy and thenByDescending functions:

```
class Human(val height: Int,val weight: Int){
    override fun toString(): String {
        return "Height = ${height}, Weight =
${weight}"
    }
}

fun main() {
    val comparators = compareBy< Human > { it.height }
    val list = listOf< Human >(
        Human (6, 14),
        Human(2, 15),
        Human(5, 55),
```

```
        Human(4, 35),
        Human(6, 85),
        Human(5, 55)
    )

    println("The Sorted first according to height then
by weight")
    val anotherComparator = comparators.thenBy {
it.weight }
    println(list.sortedWith(anotherComparator))

    println("Sorted first according to weight then by
descending order in height")
    val comparator2 = compareBy< Human > { it.weight
}.thenByDescending { it.height }
    println(list.sortedWith(comparator2))
}
```

thenComparator: This function returns a comparator that performs a comparison using the primary comparator and a function.

```
fun <D> Comparator<D>.thenComparator(
    comparison: (x: D, y: D) -> Int
): Comparator<D>
```

thenDescending: This function combines two comparator, the second of which is used only when the values according to the first comparator are equal, and sorts the elements in descending order.

```
infix fun <D> Comparator<D>.thenDescending(
    comparator: Comparator<in D>
): Comparator<D>
```

Example of thenComparator and thenDescending functions:

```
fun main(){
    val lists = listOf<Pairs<String,Int>>(
        Pairs("D",3),
        Pairs("C",1),
        Pairs("E",345),
        Pairs("P",20),
        Pairs("S",0),
```

```
        Pairs("B",0)
    )

    val comparators = compareBy<Pair<String,Int>>
{ it.first }
        .thenComparator({x,y -> compareValues
(x.second,y.second)})
    println("The Pairs sorted by String then by
Integers")
    println(lists.sortedWith(comparators))
    val anotherComparator =
compareBy<Pairs<String,Int>> { it.second }
    val anotherComparator2 =
compareBy<Pairs<String,Int>>{it.first}
    println("The Pairs sorted by Integers then by
Strings in Descending order")
    println(list.sortedWith(anotherComparator.thenDesc
ending(anotherComparator2)))
}
```

CONCLUSION

In this chapter, we covered collections where we learned what collection is, including ArrayList, listOf, and setOf, and we also covered mutableSetOf, HashSet, and Map in Kotlin. Moreover, we covered annotations, reflection, operator overloading, and destructing declaration. Also, we learned about the equality equation and comparator.

CHAPTER 7

Android Development with Kotlin

➤ Create a project in Android Studio using Kotlin

➤ Install AVD

➤ Android animation

➤ Fade In/Out

➤ Menus

We covered collection with ArrayList, listOf, setOf, mutableSet, and Map in Chapter 6. Moreover, we covered annotations, reflection, overloading, and comparator. This chapter will discuss installing Android Studio, installing AVD, animation, and menus.

KOTLIN FOR ANDROID

Kotlin is a cross platform programming language that may use as an alternative to Java for developing Android apps. When compared to Java, Kotlin is significantly easier for novices to learn, and this Kotlin Android Tutorial may also be used as an "entry point" for Android App Development. Google sponsors Kotlin, which was introduced as one of the official languages for Android development in 2017. Kotlin is a multiplatform programming language that can readily execute on a Java Virtual Machine.

DOI: 10.1201/9781003311904-7   **261**

How to Install and Configure Android Studio for Kotlin Development

To create an Android application with Kotlin, we'll need an Android application development IDE like Android Studio. Android Studio is an IDE that lets us create applications on a single platform. We can get the Android Studio package from the official Android Studio website: https://developer.android.com/studio/index.html

- Java must be installed on our PC before we can install Android Studio.

- After downloading Android Studio, launch it and install it. Follow the installation instructions.

- Select Next to proceed.

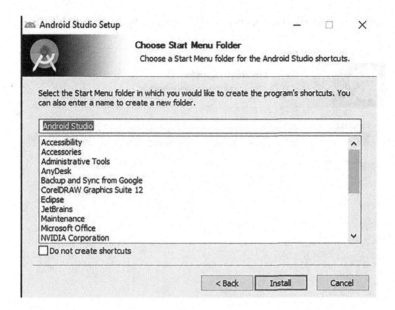

- Browse the JDK path and click Next.

- Analyze the component that we wish to install.

- Indicate the location of the Android SDK installation.

- To utilize emulator instances, set the maximum RAM size.

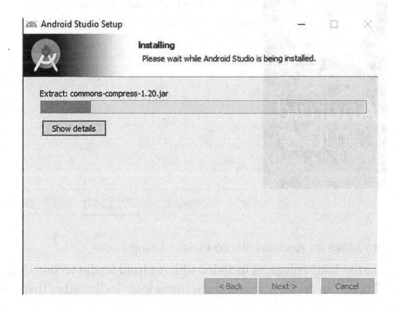

- Android Studio has been installed successfully on our machine.

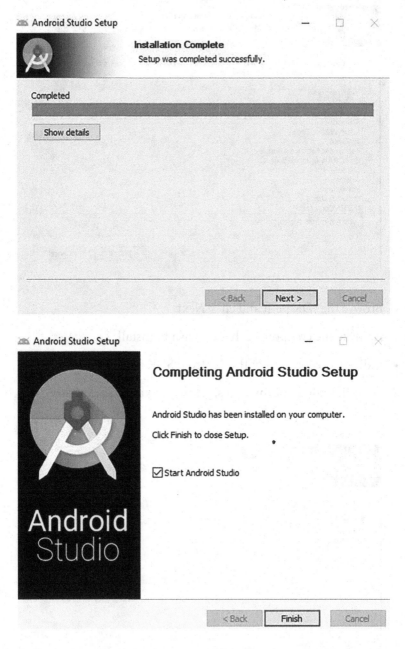

How to Make an Android Studio Project Using Kotlin

Because the Kotlin plugin is included with Android Studio versions higher than 3.0, we can create Android applications with Kotlin rather than Java.

The procedures for creating a new project in the Kotlin programming language are discussed below:

- **Step 1:** From the Welcome to Android Studio page, choose to Start a New Android Studio Project.

- **Step 2:** Click the Next button after selecting Empty Activity.

- **Step 3:** Here, we write the name of our application and choose Kotlin as the language for the project. Then, to begin the project, click the Finish button.

- **Step 4:** Finally, our newly created project with a variable number of files opens.

HELLOO WORLD APP IN KOTLIN

- Let's create our helloo world app in Android Studio using the Kotlin programming language. Run Android Studio and choose the "Start a new Android Studio project" option to create an Android application.

- Provide a name for our application ("Helloo World" in my instance) and click the "Include Kotlin support" and proceed.

- Click Next after selecting the API level for the Android application.

- Select the Activity type and then click the Next button.

- activities_main.xml

  Add the following code to the activities_main.xml file in the layout folder.

```xml
<?xml version="1.0" encoding="utf-8"?>
<android.support.constraint.ConstraintLayout
xmlns:android="http://schemas.android.com/apk/res/
android"
    xmlns:app="http://schemas.android.com/apk/
res-auto"
    xmlns:tools="http://schemas.android.com/tools"
    android:layout_width="match_parent"
    android:layout_height="match_parent"
    tools:context="example.app.javatpoint.
hellooworld.MainActivity">
```

```
<TextView
    android:layout_width="wrap_content"
    android:layout_height="wrap_content"
    android:text="Hellooo World!"
    app:layout_constraintBottom_toBottomOf=
"parent"
    app:layout_constraintLeft_toLeftOf=
"parent"
    app:layout_constraintRight_toRightOf=
"parent"
    app:layout_constraintTop_toTopOf=
"parent" />

</android.support.constraint.ConstraintLayout>
```

- MainActivities.kt

   In the example.app.javatpoint.helloworld package, create a MainActivities.kt file, and add the following code.

```
package example.app.javatpoint.hellooworld

import android.support.v7.app.AppCompatActivity
import android.os.Bundle

class MainActivity : AppCompatActivity() {

    override fun onCreate(savedInstanceState:
Bundle?) {
        super.onCreate(savedInstanceState)
        setContentView(R.layout.activity_main)
    }
}
```

- Now run our app.

HOW TO SET UP AN ANDROID VIRTUAL DEVICE (AVD)

To execute the program in android development, we need an android smartphone. As a result, Android Studio's developers give the option to install an AVD to operate it. This part will go through how to set up an AVD.

To install AVD, follow the following steps:

- **Step 1:** Select Tools > AVD Manager from the Menu.

- **Step 2:** Next, select Create Virtual Device.

- **Step 3:** Popup window will appear, and we will pick the category Phone since we are making an android app for a mobile phone and the model of mobile phone we wish to install.

- **Step 4:** Here, we pick the Android version to download, such as Q, Pie, Oreo, and so on, and then click the Next button.

- **Step 5:** To complete the installation, click the Finish button.

- **Step 6:** Now, we can pick the virtual device we wish to use as an emulator and press the run button.

- **Step 7:** Our virtual device is finally ready to execute our Android app.

KOTLIN ANIMATIONS FOR ANDROID

Animation is a technique in which a group of images is mixed in a certain way and processed to look like moving images. Building animations provide the appearance that on-screen things are living. Android includes a plethora of tools that can assist us in creating animations with reasonable simplicity. So, in this section, we'll learn how to make animations using Kotlin. The following are some properties that we use when developing xml code.

Attributes Table:

XML Attributes	Description
android:duration	It is used to determine the length of the animation to run.
android:fromAlpha	It is the initial alpha value for the animation, where 1.0 indicates entirely opaque, and 0.0 implies fully transparent.
android:toAlpha	It is the final alpha value.
android:id	Sets the view's unique id.
android:fromYDelta	The Y coordinate modification will be applied at the start of the animation.
android:toYDelta	The Y coordinate modification will be applied at the conclusion of the animation.

(Continued)

XML Attributes	Description
android:startOffset	There is a delay when an animation runs (in milliseconds) after the start time is achieved.
android:pivotX	It denotes the X-axis coordinates for zooming out from the starting point.
android:pivotY	It denotes the Y-axis coordinates for zooming out from the starting location.
android:fromXScale	Offset of the starting X size.
android:fromYScale	Offset of the starting Y size.
android:toXScale	X size offset at the end.
android:toYScale	Y size offset at the end.
android:fromDegrees	In degrees, the starting angular position.
android:toDegrees	In degrees, the final angular position.
android:interpolator	An interpolator defines rate of change of an animation.

To begin, we will develop a new Android application. Then we'll make some animations.

If we have previously established the project, skip step 1.

Make a New Project

- Open Android Studio.

- Go to File => New => New Project to start a new project.

- Then, pick Empty Activity and press the next button.

  - DynamicEditTextKotlin is the name of the program.

  - Select the minimal SDK that we require; in this case, we have chosen 21 as the minimum SDK.

  - Select Kotlin as the language and click the Finish button.

If we performed the steps above correctly, we should have a newly created project.

Following the creation of the project, we will alter the XML files. In the XML file, we will build one TextView in which all of the animations will be done and eight Buttons for each of the eight animations.

Change the activity_main.xml File

Add code to the res/layout/activity_main.xml file.

XML:

```xml
<?xml version="1.0" encoding="utf-8"?>
<RelativeLayout xmlns:android="http://schemas.android.
com/apk/res/android"
    xmlns:tools="http://schemas.android.com/tools"
    android:layout_width="match_parent"
    android:layout_height="match_parent"
    tools:context=".MainActivity">
    <TextView
        android:id="@+id/textView"
        android:layout_width="match_parent"
        android:layout_height="match_parent"
        android:layout_above="@+id/linearLayout"
        android:gravity="left"
        android:text="Peeks for Peeks"
        android:textSize="33sp"
        android:textColor="@color/colorPrimaryDark"
        android:textStyle="bold" />
    <LinearLayout
        android:id="@+id/linearLayout"
        android:layout_width="match_parent"
        android:layout_height="wrap_content"
        android:layout_alignParentBottom="true"
        android:orientation="horizontal">
        <LinearLayout
            android:layout_width="match_parent"
            android:layout_height="wrap_content"
            android:orientation=" vertical "
            android:weightSum="3">
            <Button
                android:id="@+id/fade_in"
                android:layout_width="0dp"
                android:layout_height="match_parent"
                android:layout_weight="2"
                android:text="Fade In"
                android:textAllCaps="false" />
            <Button
                android:id="@+id/fade_out"
                android:layout_width="0dp"
                android:layout_height="match_parent"
                android:layout_weight="2"
```

```xml
        android:text="Fade Out"
        android:textAllCaps="false" />
</LinearLayout>
<LinearLayout
    android:layout_width="match_parent"
    android:layout_height="wrap_content"
    android:orientation="horizontal"
    android:weightSum="1">
    <Button
        android:id="@+id/zoom_in"
        android:layout_width="0dp"
        android:layout_height="match_parent"
        android:layout_weight="3"
        android:text="Zoom In"
        android:textAllCaps="false" />
    <Button
        android:id="@+id/zoom_out"
        android:layout_width="0dp"
        android:layout_height="match_parent"
        android:layout_weight="2"
        android:text="Zoom Out"
        android:textAllCaps="false" />
</LinearLayout>
<LinearLayout
    android:layout_width="match_parent"
    android:layout_height="wrap_content"
    android:orientation=" vertical "
    android:weightSum="3">
    <Button
        android:id="@+id/slide_down"
        android:layout_width="0dp"
        android:layout_height="match_parent"
        android:layout_weight="2"
        android:text="Slide Down"
        android:textAllCaps="false" />
    <Button
        android:id="@+id/slide_up"
        android:layout_width="0dp"
        android:layout_height="match_parent"
        android:layout_weight="2"
        android:text="Slide Up"
        android:textAllCaps="false" />
</LinearLayout>
```

```
<LinearLayout
    android:layout_width="match_parent"
    android:layout_height="wrap_content"
    android:orientation="vertical"
    android:weightSum="1">
    <Button
        android:id="@+id/bounce"
        android:layout_width="0dp"
        android:layout_height="match_parent"
        android:layout_weight="3"
        android:text="Bounce"
        android:textAllCaps="false" />
    <Button
        android:id="@+id/rotate"
        android:layout_width="0dp"
        android:layout_height="match_parent"
        android:layout_weight="3"
        android:text="Rotate"
        android:textAllCaps="false" />
</LinearLayout>
    </LinearLayout>
</RelativeLayout>
```

We will develop XML files for animations when we have modified the layout. So, initially, we'll make a folder called anim.

In this folder, we place the XML files that will utilize to generate the animations. To accomplish this, go to app/res, right-click, and then pick Android Resource Directory, and name it anim.

bounce.xml

XML: The text in this animation bounces like a ball.

```
<?xml version="1.0" encoding="utf-8"?>
<set
    xmlns:android="http://schemas.android.com/apk/res/
android"
    android:interpolator="@android:anim/
linear_interpolator"
    android:fillAfter="true">
    <translate
        android:fromYDelta="90%"
        android:toYDelta="-25%"
        android:duration="320" />
    <translate
```

```
        android:startOffset="550"
        android:fromYDelta="-30%"
        android:toYDelta="20%"
        android:duration="140" />
    <translate
        android:startOffset="1100"
        android:fromYDelta="15%"
        android:toYDelta="0"
        android:duration="120" />
</set>
```

fade in.xml

The text will appear from the background in the Fade In motion.

XML:

```
<?xml version="1.0" encoding="utf-8"?>
<set xmlns:android="http://schemas.android.com/apk/
res/android"
    android:interpolator="@android:anim/
linear_interpolator">
    <alpha
        android:duration="1200"
        android:fromAlpha="0.2"
        android:toAlpha="2.0" />
</set>
```

fade_out.xml

The color of text gets faded out for a set period of time in the Fade Out animation.

XML:

```
<?xml version="1.0" encoding="utf-8"?>
<set xmlns:android="http://schemas.android.com/apk/
res/android"
    android:interpolator="@android:anim/
linear_interpolator">
    <alpha
        android:duration="1200"
        android:fromAlpha="2.0"
        android:toAlpha="0.2" />
</set>
```

rotate.xml

The text is rotated for a certain period of time in rotate animation.

XML:

```xml
<?xml version="1.0" encoding="utf-8"?>
<rotate xmlns:android="http://schemas.android.com/apk/
res/android"
    android:duration="1200"
    android:fromDegrees="0"
    android:interpolator="@android:anim/
linear_interpolator"
    android:pivotX="60%"
    android:pivotY="60%"
    android:startOffset="0"
    android:toDegrees="320" />
```

slide_down.xml

The text in this animation will come from top to bottom.

XML:

```xml
<?xml version="1.0" encoding="utf-8"?>
<set xmlns:android="http://schemas.android.com/apk/
res/android">
    <translate
        android:duration="1200"
        android:fromYDelta="-90%"
        android:toYDelta="0" />
</set>
```

slide_up.xml

The text in this animation will go from bottom to the top.

XML:

```xml
<set xmlns:android="http://schemas.android.com/apk/
res/android">
    <translate
        android:duration="1200"
        android:fromYDelta="0"
        android:toYDelta="-90%" />
</set>
```

zoom_in.xml

The text in this animation will seem larger for a certain amount of time.

XML:

```xml
<?xml version="1.0" encoding="utf-8"?>
<set xmlns:android="http://schemas.android.com/apk/
res/android"
    android:fillAfter="true">
    <scale xmlns:android="http://schemas.android.com/
apk/res/android"
        android:duration="1200"
        android:fromXScale="2"
        android:fromYScale="2"
        android:pivotX="60%"
        android:pivotY="60%"
        android:toXScale="2.5"
        android:toYScale="2.5">
    </scale>
</set>
```

zoom_out.xml

The text in this animation will seem smaller for a certain length of time.

XML:

```xml
<?xml version="1.0" encoding="utf-8"?>
<set xmlns:android="http://schemas.android.com/apk/
res/android"
    android:fillAfter="true" >
    <scale
        xmlns:android="http://schemas.android.com/apk/
res/android"
        android:duration="1200"
        android:fromXScale="2.0"
        android:fromYScale="2.0"
        android:pivotX="60%"
        android:pivotY="60%"
        android:toXScale="0.7"
        android:toYScale="0.7" >
    </scale>
</set>
```

Following the creation of all xml animations, we'll make MainActivity.

Create MainActivity.kt File

Open app/src/main/java/peeksforpeeks. AnimationsInKotlin/Main Activity.kt file and add the below code into it.

```
package peeksforpeeks.animationsinkotlin
import androidx.appcompat.app.AppCompatActivity
import android.os.Bundle
import android.os.Handler
import android.view.View
import android.view.animation.AnimationUtils
import kotlinx.android.synthetic.main.activity_main.*

class MainActivity : AppCompatActivity() {
    override fun onCreate(savedInstanceState: Bundle?) {
        super.onCreate(savedInstanceState)
        setContentView(C.layout.activity_main)
        fade_in.setOnClickListener {
            textView.visibility = View.VISIBLE
            val animationFadeIn = AnimationUtils.
loadAnimation(this, C.anim.fade_in)
            textView.startAnimation(animationFadeIn)
        }
        fade_out.setOnClickListener {
            val animationFadeOut = AnimationUtils.
loadAnimation(this, C.anim.fade_out)
            textView.startAnimation(animationFadeOut)
            Handler().postDelayed({
                textView.visibility = View.GONE
            }, 1200)
        }
        zoom_in.setOnClickListener {
            val animationZoomIn = AnimationUtils.
loadAnimation(this, C.anim.zoom_in)
            textView.startAnimation(animationZoomIn)
        }
        zoom_out.setOnClickListener {
            val animationZoomOut = AnimationUtils.
loadAnimation(this, C.anim.zoom_out)
            textView.startAnimation(animationZoomOut)
        }
        slide_down.setOnClickListener {
            val animationSlideDown = AnimationUtils.
loadAnimation(this, C.anim.slide_in)
```

```
            textView.startAnimation(animationSlideDown)
        }
        slide_up.setOnClickListener {
            val animationSlideUp = AnimationUtils.
loadAnimation(this, C.anim.slide_out)
            textView.startAnimation(animationSlideUp)
        }
        bounce.setOnClickListener {
            val animationBounce = AnimationUtils.
loadAnimation(this, C.anim.bounce)
            textView.startAnimation(animationBounce)
        }
        rotate.setOnClickListener {
            val animationRotate = AnimationUtils.
loadAnimation(this, C.anim.rotate)
            textView.startAnimation(animationRotate)
        }
    }
}
```

Because the AndroidManifest.xml file is so vital in Android applications, the code for the manifest file is provided here.

AndroidManifest.xml File

```xml
<?xml version="1.0" encoding="utf-8"?>
<manifest xmlns:android="http://schemas.android.com/
apk/res/android"
    package="peeksforpeeks.animationsinkotlin">

    <application
        android:allowBackup="true"
        android:icon="@mipmap/ic_launcher"
        android:label="@string/app_name"
        android:roundIcon="@mipmap/ic_launcher_round"
        android:supportsRtl="true"
        android:theme="@style/AppTheme">
        <activity android:name=".MainActivity">
            <intent-filter>
                <action android:name="android.intent.
action.MAIN" />
                <category android:name="android.
intent.category.LAUNCHER" />
            </intent-filter>
```

```
      </activity>
    </application>
</manifest>
```

KOTLIN ANDROID FADE IN/OUT

Animations in Android are graphics that are introduced to make the user interface more dynamic, clear, and appealing. Fade-in and fade-out animations are used to change the appearance of any view over a specific period of time so that the user is alerted to changes in our program.

In this post, the section we will look at how to make a Fade In/Out animation in Kotlin.

XML Attributes	Description
android:duration	It is used to specify the length of the animation.
android:fromAlpha	It is the initial alpha value for the animation, with 1.0 indicating complete opacity and 0.0 indicating complete transparency.
android:toAlpha	It is the final alpha value.
android:id	Sets the view's unique id.

The first step is to open Android Studio and create a new project. Follow these steps to accomplish this:

- Click File, then New, then New Project, then name it whatever we like.

- Then, choose Kotlin language support and press the next button.

- Choose the minimum SDKs we need.

- Choose Empty activity, and then click Finish.

- Following that, we must create our layout. We'll need to use the XML file for this. Navigate to app > res > layout and copy the following code:

Modify activity_main.xml File

```
<?xml version="1.0" encoding="utf-8"?>
<RelativeLayout xmlns:android="http://schemas.android.
com/apk/res/android"
                xmlns:app="http://schemas.android.com/
apk/res-auto"
                xmlns:tools="http://schemas.android.com/
tools"
```

```
        android:layout_width="match_parent"
        android:layout_height="match_parent"
        tools:context=".MainActivity" android:or
ientation="vertical">
    <TextView
        android:id="@+id/textView"
        android:layout_width="wrap_content"
        android:layout_height="wrap_content"
        android:text="PeeksofPeeks"
        android:layout_centerInParent="true"
        android:textSize="33sp"
        android:textStyle="bold" />

    <Button
        android:id="@+id/fade_in"
        android:layout_width="90dp"
        android:layout_height="wrap_content"
        android:text="Fade In"
        android:layout_marginTop="150dp"
        android:layout_marginLeft="90dp" />
    <Button
        android:id="@+id/fade_out"
        android:layout_width="120dp"
        android:layout_height="wrap_content"
        android:layout_marginTop="130dp"
        android:layout_toRightOf="@+id/fade_in"
        android:text="Fade Out"
        android:textAllCaps="false" />
</RelativeLayout>
```

Add an anim Folder

In this folder, we'll put the XML files that will utilize to generate the animations. To accomplish this, go to app/res, right-click, and then pick Android Resource Directory, and name it anim.

Right, click this anim folder again, this time selecting Animation resource file and naming it fade_in. Similarly, create fade_out.xml and paste the code below.

fade_in.xml:

```
<?xml version="1.0" encoding="utf-8"?>
<set xmlns:android="http://schemas.android.com/apk/
res/android">
```

```
        android:interpolator="@android:anim/
linear_interpolator">
    <alpha
        android:duration="2300"
        android:fromAlpha="0.2"
        android:toAlpha="2.0" />
</set>
```

fade_out.xml:

```
<?xml version="1.0" encoding="utf-8"?>
<set xmlns:android="http://schemas.android.com/apk/
res/android">
    android:interpolator="@android:anim/
linear_interpolator">
    <alpha
        android:duration="2200"
        android:fromAlpha="2.0"
        android:toAlpha="0.2" />
</set>
```

Change the MainActivity.kt File

Make the following modifications to app/src/main/java/ourPackageName/ MainActivity.kt:

```
package com.peeksforpeeks.myfirstapp
import androidx.appcompat.app.AppCompatActivity
import android.os.Bundle
import android.os.Handler
import android.view.View
import android.view.animation.AnimationUtils
import kotlinx.android.synthetic.main.activity_main.*
class MainActivity : AppCompatActivity() {

    override fun onCreate(savedInstanceState: Bundle?) {
        super.onCreate(savedInstanceState)
        setContentView(R.layout.activity_main)
        //setting the button onClickListener
        fade_in.setOnClickListener {
        textView.visibility = View.VISIBLE
        //loading custom made animations
        val animations = AnimationUtils.
loadAnimation(this, C.anim.fade_in)
```

```kotlin
        //starting the animations
        textView.startAnimation(animations)
    }
    fade_out.setOnClickListener {
        val animations = AnimationUtils.
loadAnimation(this, C.anim.fade_out)
        textView.startAnimation(animations)
        //textview will be invisible after specified
amount
        // of time elapses, here it is 1200
milliseconds
        Handler().postDelayed({
            textView.visibility = View.GONE
        }, 1200)
    }
}
}
```

AndroidManifest.xml File

```xml
<?xml version="1.0" encoding="utf-8"?>
<manifest xmlns:android="http://schemas.android.com/
apk/res/android"
          package="x.apps.fadeinout">

    <application
            android:allowBackup="true"
            android:icon="@mipmap/ic_launcher"
            android:label="@string/app_name"
            android:roundIcon="@mipmap/
ic_launcher_round"
            android:supportsRtl="true"
            android:theme="@style/AppTheme">
        <activity android:name=".MainActivity">
            <intent-filter>
                <action android:name="android.intent.
action.MAIN"/>
                <category android:name="android.
intent.category.LAUNCHER"/>
            </intent-filter>
        </activity>
    </application>
</manifest>
```

MENUS FOR ANDROID

The menu is an essential UI component in Android that provides certain common functions throughout the application. The Menu allows the user to have a smooth and consistent experience across the program.

To use a menu, we must define it in a separate XML file and then use that file in our program based on our needs. In addition, we can utilize menu APIs to represent user actions and other options in our Android app activities.

How Can We Define a Menu in an XML File?

Android Studio provides a standard XML format for kinds of menus to specify menu elements. Instead of writing code, we can describe the menu and its items in an XML menu resource and load the menu resource as a menu object in the activity or fragment used in our Android application.

To define the menu, we need to create a new folder within our project directory (res/menu) and add a new XML file with the following components.

The example of defining a menu in an XML file (menu example.xml) is shown below:

```xml
<?xml version="1.0" encoding="utf-8"?>
<menu xmlns:android="http:// schemas.android.com/apk/
res/android">
    <item android:id="@+id/mail"
        android:icon="@drawable/ic_mail"
        android:title="@string/mail" />
    <item android:id="@+id/upload"
        android:icon="@drawable/ic_upload"
        android:title="@string/upload"
        android:showAsAction="ifRoom" />
    <item android:id="@+id/share"
        android:icon="@drawable/ic_share"
        android:title="@string/share" />
</menu>
```

- **<Menu>:** The XML file's root element that helps define the Menu and holds various items.

- **<item>:** It is used to generate a single menu item. It also has nested Menu> elements to form a submenu.

- **<group>:** It is optional and unnoticed for item> elements to classify menu items so that they can share features such as active status and visibility.

activity_main.xml: If we wish to include a submenu in a menu item, we must consist of a menu> element as child of an item>.

The following is an example of defining a submenu in a menu item:

```xml
<?xml version="1.0" encoding="utf-8"?>
<menu xmlns:android="http:// schemas.android.com/apk/
res/android">
    <item android:id="@+id/file"
        android:title="@string/file" >
        <!-- "file"submenu -->
        <menu>
            <item android:id="@+id/create_new"
                android:title="@string/create_new" />
            <item android:id="@+id/open"
                android:title="@string/open" />
        </menu>
    </item>
</menu>
```

Different Sorts of Menus in Android

There are three types of menus accessible in Android for defining a collection of options and actions in our android applications.

The Android application's menus are as follows:

- **Android Options Menu:** In an Android application, a menu is a primary collection of menu items that is important for activities that have a worldwide impact on the searching application.

- **Android Context Menu:** Android Context Menu is a floating menu that shows only when the user clicks on an element for an extended period of time. It is ideal for components that affect the chosen content or context frame.

- **Android Popup Menu:** The Android Popup Menu shows a list of items in a vertical list to the view that activated the Menu and is handy for providing an overflow of actions connected to specific content.

Kotlin Progress Alerts for Android

This section will teach us how to use Kotlin to develop a simple Progress Notification (Indeterminate progress indicator and Fixed-duration progress indicator) for Android.

Before we begin, let us define the components of an Android notification:

- **Small Icon:** This is required and may be set using setSmallIcon ().

- **Application Name:** The system provides the application name.

- **Time Stamp:** This is the provided by system but can be changed.

- **Large Icon:** This is optional, may be configured with setLargeIcon ().

- **Title:** This is an optional title, which may be specified using setContentTitle ().

- **Text:** This is optional and may be set using setContentText ().

Take Note of Notification Channels

Since the release of Android version 8 (Android Oreo), it has been mandatory to categorize all alerts into "channels" for the convenience of both users and developers.

Because we only need to construct a channel once, we'll utilize a helper class called "App.kt" to accomplish the work.

App.kt:

```
package com.gfg.progressnotificationdemo
import android.app.Application
import android.app.NotificationChannel
import android.app.NotificationManager
import android.os.Build
class App : Application(){
    val channelId = "Progress Notification" as String
    override fun onCreate(){
        super.onCreate()
        createNotificationChannels()
    }
    //Check if Android version is greater than 8.
    private fun createNotificationChannels(){
        if (Build.VERSION.SDK_INT >= Build.VERSION_
CODES.O) {
```

```kotlin
        val channel1 = NotificationChannel(
            channelId,
            "Progress Notification",
    //IMPORTANCE_HIGH = shows notification as peek
notification.
    //IMPORTANCE_LOW = shows notification in the
status bar.
            NotificationManager.IMPORTANCE_HIGH
        )
        channel1.description = "Progress
Notification Channel"
        val manager = getSystemService(
            NotificationManager::class.java
        )
        manager.createNotificationChannel(chan
nel1)
    }
  }
}
```

MainActivity.kt:

```kotlin
package com.gfg.progressnotificationdemo
import android.app.PendingIntent
import android.content.Intent
import android.os.Bundle
import android.os.SystemClock
import android.view.View
import androidx.appcompat.app.AppCompatActivity
import androidx.core.app.NotificationCompat
import androidx.core.app.NotificationManagerCompat
import com.gfg.progressnotificationdemo.R.drawable
class MainActivity : AppCompatActivity(){
    private lateinit var notificationManager:
NotificationManagerCompat
    val channelId = "Progress Notification" as String
    override fun onCreate(savedInstanceState: Bundle?){
        super.onCreate(savedInstanceState)
        setContentView(R.layout.activity_main)
    //Create a Notification Manager
        notificationManager =
NotificationManagerCompat.from(this)
    }
```

```kotlin
    //Start() is called when buttons is pressed.
    public fun start(view: View){

        val intent = Intent(this, MainActivity::class.
java).apply{
            flags = Intent.FLAG_ACTIVITY_NEW_TASK or
            Intent.FLAG_ACTIVITY_CLEAR_TASK
        }
        val pendingIntent: PendingIntent =
PendingIntent.getActivity(
            this, 0, intent, 0)
    //Sets maximum progress as 90
        val progressMax = 90
    //Create notification and setting its various
attributes
        val notification =
            NotificationCompat.Builder(this,
channelId)
                .setSmallIcon(drawable.
ic_file_download)
                .setContentTitle("GeeksforGeeks")
                .setContentText("Downloading")
                .setPriority(NotificationCompat.
PRIORITY_LOW)
                .setOngoing(true)
                .setOnlyAlertOnce(true)
                .setProgress(progressMax, 0, true)
                .setContentIntent(pendingIntent)
                .setAutoCancel(true)
    //the Initial Alert
        notificationManager.notify(1, notification.
build())
        Thread(Runnable{
            SystemClock.sleep(2100)
            var progress = 0
            while (progress <= progressMax) {
                SystemClock.sleep(
                    1200
                )
                progress += 20
    //Use this to make it Fixed-duration progress
indicator notification
```

```
    //notification.setContentText(progress.
toString()+"%")
    //.setProgress(progressMax, progress, false)
    //notificationManager.notify(1, notification.
build())
            }
        notification.setContentText("Download
complete")
                .setProgress(0, 0, false)
                .setOngoing(false)
        notificationManager.notify(1,
notification.build())
        }).start()
    }
}
```

STRUCTURE OF THE ANDROID PROJECT FOLDER

Android Studio is the official IDE developed by the JetBrains community and freely given by Google to develop Android apps.

After completing the Android Architecture setup, we may construct an Android application in the studio. We must establish a new project for each sample application and comprehend the folder structure.

The Android project includes several app modules, source code files, and resource files. We will look at all of the folders and files in the Android app.

1. Manifests Folder

2. Java Folder

3. Resources (res) Folder

   • Drawable Folder

   • Layout Folder

   • Mipmap Folder

   • Values Folder

4. Gradle Scripts

Manifests Folder

The Manifests folder includes AndroidManifest.xml, which we will use to create the Android application. This file provides information about our app, such as the Android version, metadata, the states package for the Kotlin code, and other app components. It functions as a bridge between the Android operating system and our application.

AndroidManifest.xml:

```xml
<?xml version="1.0" encoding="utf-8"?>
<manifest xmlns:android="http:// schemas.android.com/
apk/res/android"
    package="peeksforpeeks.myapplication">
    <application
        android:allowBackup="true"
        android:icon="@mipmap/ic_launcher"
        android:label="@string/app_name"
        android:roundIcon="@mipmap/ic_launcher_round"
        android:supportsRtl="true"
        android:theme="@style/AppTheme">
        <activity android:name=".MainActivity">
            <intent-filter>
                <action android:name="android.intent.
action.MAIN" />

                <category android:name="android.
intent.category.LAUNCHER" />
            </intent-filter>
        </activity>
    </application>
</manifest>
```

Java Folder

The Java folder holds all of the Java and Kotlin source code (.java) files that we write throughout app development and additional test files. When we start a new Kotlin project, the class file MainActivity.kt is created automatically under the package name "peeksforpeeks.myfirstkotlinapp," as seen below.

MainActivity.kt:

```kotlin
package peeksforpeeks.myapplication
    import androidx.appcompat.app.AppCompatActivity
import android.os.Bundle
    class MainActivity : AppCompatActivity() {
    override fun onCreate(savedInstanceState: Bundle?)
```

```
    {
        super.onCreate(savedInstanceState)
            setContentView(C.layout.activity_main)
    }
}
```

Resource (res) Folder

The resource folder is the most crucial since it holds all of our android application's non-code sources like as images, XML layouts, and UI strings.

folder for res/drawables: It comprises the various types of images utilized in the application's development. For the application development, we must place all photos in the drawable folder.

Folder res/layout: The layout folder includes all of the XML layout files that we utilized to define our application's user interface. It contains the file activity main.xml.

```
<?xml version="1.0" encoding="utf-8"?>
<androidx.constraintlayout.widget.ConstraintLayout
    xmlns:android="http:// schemas.android.com/apk/
res/android"
    xmlns:app="http:// schemas.android.com/apk/res-auto"
    xmlns:tools="http:// schemas.android.com/tools"
    android:layout_width="match_parent"
    android:layout_height="match_parent"
    tools:context=".MainActivity">
    <TextView
        android:layout_width="wrap_content"
        android:layout_height="wrap_content"
        android:text="Helloo World!"
        app:layout_constraintBottom_toBottomOf=
"parent"
        app:layout_constraintLeft_toLeftOf="parent"
        app:layout_constraintRight_toRightOf="parent"
        app:layout_constraintTop_toTopOf="parent" />
</androidx.constraintlayout.widget.ConstraintLayout>
```

res/midmap folder: This folder contains launcher.xml files that specify the icons that appear on the home screen. It has multiple density types of icons depending on the device size, such as hdpi, mdpi, and xhdpi.

res/values folder: The values folder contains number of XML files that define strings, dimensions, colors, and styles. The strings.xml file, which includes the resources, is one of the most crucial.

```
<resources>
    <string name="app_name">NameOfTheApplication</
string>
    <string name="checked">Checked</string>
    <string name="unchecked">Unchecked</string>
</resources>
```

Gradle Scripts Folder

Gradle is an automated build system that includes several files that create a build configuration that can apply to all modules in our application. Buildscripts are used in build.gradle (Project), and plugins and implementations are used in build.gradle (Module) to create settings that can apply to all of our application modules.

CONCLUSION

In this chapter, we covered Android development in Kotlin where we also covered how to create the project in Android Studio and install AVD. We also learned Kolin's animation, menus, progress notification, and project folder structure.

Appraisal

Kotlin is a programming language released in 2011 by JetBrains, the official creator of the most intelligent Java IDE, Intellij IDEA. This general-purpose programming language is heavily statically typed and runs on the JVM. Google declared Kotlin to be an official language for Android development in 2017. Kotlin is an open-source programming language that mixes object-oriented programming with functional capabilities to provide a one-of-a-kind platform.

KOTLIN ONLINE COMPILER

We have created a Kotlin Online Compiler that allows us to modify and execute code straight from our browser using our simple editor. Try clicking the icon run button to execute the following Kotlin code to produce the standard "Helloo, World!" message.

```
fun main() {
    var string: String1  = "Helloo, World!"  //
defining variable
    println("$string1")
}
```

KOTLIN VS. JAVA

The subject of whether to use Kotlin versus Java for new development has been a hot topic in the Android community since the Google I/O announcement. The issue goes back to February 2016, when Kotlin 1.0 was released. The quick answer is that Kotlin code is safer and uses fewer resources than Java code. Because Kotlin and Java files may coexist in Android apps, Kotlin is beneficial not just for new apps but also for expanding existing Java apps.

DOI: 10.1201/9781003311904-8

The only compelling justification we've seen for using Java over Kotlin is for total Android programming novices. Given that most Android documentation and examples have historically been written in Java, they might be challenging. Converting Java to Kotlin with Android Studio, on the other hand, is as simple as putting the Java code into a Kotlin file.

The benefits of Kotlin are compelling for practically everyone else undertaking Android programming. A Java developer will typically spend a few hours learning Kotlin – a modest price to pay to remove null reference issues, enable extension functions, support functional programming, and add coroutines. The standard rough estimate implies a 40% reduction in the number of lines of code when switching from Java to Kotlin.

WHAT ARE THE BENEFITS OF KOTLIN?

Kotlin was created due to Lead Developer Dmitry Jemerov's search for functionality that he couldn't find in Java. Scala is another language that runs on the JVM; it came close, but compiling took too long.

Jemerov desired a language with all of the characteristics of more recent programming languages, which could operate on the JVM and compile as quickly as Java. As a result, he developed his language, Kotlin.

Kotlin was supposed to be a substitute for Java on the Android operating system. In 2019, Google ultimately agreed with Jemerov and most Android developers and proclaimed that Kotlin was the ideal language for Android app development eight years after it was launched.

Here are some of the reasons why developers choose Kotlin over Java:

- Kotlin is succinct, which saves time spent creating boilerplate code in Java.

- A script may use to convert a Java file to a Kotlin file.

- There is no runtime overhead with Kotlin. Adding features to a language can sometimes result in increased overhead, which reduces efficiency. Not the case with Kotlin.

- Kotlin has a sizable user base. If we get stuck, we may obtain support from other developers on coding forums and social networks.

- Kotlin makes asynchronous programming more accessible. Making asynchronous network and database calls in Java is clunky and inconvenient. Coroutines in Kotlin make asynchronous programming efficient and straightforward.

- Nulls are handled in Kotlin. If we don't plan for a null in Java, it might cause a program to crash. To avoid these problems, we may add a simple operator to variables' null field in Kotlin.

- Kotlin can operate on a variety of systems. Kotlin can run everywhere Java can, allowing you to create cross-platform programs.

- It is simple to transition to Kotlin. Because Kotlin is entirely compatible with Java, we do not need to replace all of our code at once. We may gradually move an application to Kotlin.

WHAT IS THE USE OF KOTLIN?

Kotlin is intended to operate on a Java Virtual Machine and can coexist alongside Java. Although Kotlin began as a language for Android development, its features soon expanded beyond the Java community, and it is now utilized for a wide range of applications.

Android Development

Kotlin is the recommended language for Android development because it allows developers to write more concise, expressive, and secure code. Android Studio, the official IDE for Android development, fully supports it, so we can receive the same sort of code completion and type checking to assist us in creating Kotlin code as we can with Java.

Because more people now access the Internet via mobile phones, most companies must have a mobile presence. Because Android accounts for more than 70% of the mobile phone market, Kotlin developers would be in great demand even if Kotlin was solely used for Android development. It may, however, be used for much more.

Back-End Web Development

Back-end web development in Java is standard, with popular frameworks such as Spring. However, since it was simpler to work with, Kotlin made inroads into server-side web development.

The language's contemporary capabilities enable web developers to create apps that expand fast on commodity hardware. Because Kotlin and Java are compatible, we may gradually migrate an application to use Kotlin one file at a time while the remainder of the program continues to use Java.

Kotlin also works with Spring and other frameworks, so migrating to Kotlin does not need a complete overhaul of our existing code. Google,

Amazon, and many more organizations have already replaced Java in their server-side code with Kotlin.

Full-Stack Web Development

Kotlin makes sense for server-side web development. After all, Java has been around since the beginning. We may still use Kotlin for front-end programming using Kotlin/JS.

Kotlin/JS gives developers type-safe access to a sophisticated browser and online APIs. Full-Stack developers need to be familiar with Kotlin. They can create front-end code in the same language as back-end code, and it will be compiled to JavaScript to execute in the browser.

Data Science

Data scientists have long used Java to crunch information, discover patterns, and make predictions, so it seems to reason that Kotlin will find a home in this field as well.

Data scientists can utilize all of the standard Java libraries that they are accustomed to using in Java projects, but they must develop their code in Kotlin. Jupyter and Zeppelin, two tools that many data scientists regularly utilize for data visualization and exploratory study, support Kotlin.

MULTI-PLATFORM MOBILE DEVELOPMENT

Kotlin multi-platform mobile is a software development kit for building cross-platform mobile applications. This implies that we'll be able to generate apps that operate not only on Android phones but also on iPhones and the Apple Watch from a single Kotlin codebase.

WHY SHOULD WE LEARN KOTLIN NOW?

Everyone desires their app. However, getting it off the ground might be a complex undertaking if we don't know-how. There are about 2.55 million applications on the Google Play store, and the number is growing all the time. We should all study Kotlin whether we're just starting or seeking to increase our knowledge. You may wonder why we should study Kotlin instead of investing in other programming languages. So, let us break it down.

The creation of Android apps is not going away anytime soon. With fewer entry points to the ecosystem than iOS, Android OS users have consistently increased over the last decade. Android has maintained and increased its dominant market share of smartphone operating systems for the previous decade, which now stands at 73%. The reasons for learning Kotlin over Java, for example, are self-evident.

Simple to Grasp

One of the significant considerations when learning a new language is its complexity. Understanding and mastering Kotlin will be almost straight-forward for anyone with prior development expertise. Kotlin's syntax and design are simple to grasp while still quite powerful. This is one of the critical reasons why Kotlin has surpassed Java as the preferred language for creating Android apps.

Interoperable with Java

One of the most challenging elements of learning a new language is that there will be a lot of migration if we have an established project or work as part of a team. The beauty of Kotlin is that it is entirely compatible with Java. We don't have to quit using Java right now or change all of our code; we may utilize both. While doing so, add more and more Kotlin progres-sively to ensure a seamless conversion.

Extensions

Extension methods allow for adding functionality to existing classes with-out completely rewriting them in Kotlin. This means we can use Kotlin's rich features without having to lose all of the skills we've acquired while developing current apps. It enables the recovery of views from Activities, Fragments, and Views in an incredibly smooth manner. It also generates a local view cache.

Null Pointer Exceptions Are No Longer an Issue

One of the biggest concerns with Java was the Null Pointer Exception, which caused Android apps to break regularly. This is a problem that almost every developer has encountered. Kotlin, on the other hand, is null safe; hence, this error does not occur. This benefit alone has per-suaded many developers to make the transition, and if we've seen it, we'll understand.

Dependable and Secure

Not only is there no Null Pointer Exception, but Kotlin is considerably more secure and stable than Java. Because of avoidable issues, the likeli-hood of faults and mistakes in Kotlin is much smaller. And any problems that do arise are identified during the compilation process, giving it a significant reliability advantage over Java.

Strong Support

Kotlin has been around for a long time despite its current popularity, and developers have made the most of this. Support has been available, and Kotlin is prospering with the flood of new developers, not to mention that Google officially endorses it. Google announced formal Kotlin support at Google I/O in May 2017. And the community is there to assist you in making the most of it.

There Are Several Tools Available to Help Improve Your Skills

Aside from the fact that Kotlin is typically relatively easy to pick up and learn, there are many helpful resources to get us started.

Multiplatform Kotlin

JetBrains just announced Kotlin Multiplatform in 2020, which is an extension of the language that allows it to be used for more than just Android app development. Kotlin Multiplatform allows developers to create apps for both iOS and Android using a single codebase. This has the potential to be a game changer, propelling Kotlin to the forefront of programming languages.

KOTLIN MULTIPLATFORM ADVANTAGES

1. **Modular integration:** Probably the most significant advantage of Kotlin is that it is an SDK rather than a framework. This implies that teams with current apps may add a module or move a small portion to test its potential without making a significant investment. This significantly aids Kotlin in addressing the most significant barrier to migrating to a new codebase.

2. **Ease of learning:** Kotlin is already a popular programming language, and its syntax is remarkably similar to those of other popular languages such as Swift and Java. This also lowers the entrance hurdle and encourages developers to use Kotlin as an alternative.

3. **A unified codebase for business logic:** Cross-platform development solutions, by definition, enable you to use a single code base across

several systems, and Kotlin Multiplatform is no exception. The benefit of using Kotlin is that it allows you to share functionality and libraries underneath the UI layer. This allows developers to interact directly with their native environment (iOS/Android).

4. **Native UI experience:** Unlike other cross-platform choices such as Flutter, Kotlin Multiplatform does not require developers to adhere to its UI. It enables you to fully leverage native UI components as though you were building natively.

5. **Improved performance:** The use of native components allows Kotlin-written apps to perform as well as natively produced apps. This is a highly sought-after benefit for many developers wanting to create an MVP.

JOBS IN KOTLIN

Kotlin is in great demand, and all big corporations are using it to construct online and mobile apps.

A Kotlin developer's yearly compensation is roughly $130,000. However, it varies depending on where you live. The following are some of the top firms that use Kotlin:

- Google
- Amazon
- Netflix
- Pinterest
- Uber
- Trello
- Coursera
- Basecamp
- Corda
- JetBrains

WHAT ARE THE DUTIES OF A KOTLIN DEVELOPER?

- Using Kotlin, you can plan, create, and construct apps and software.
- Participating at all stages of the development cycle.
- When necessary, features are tested and modified.
- Ensure that designs adhere to the specifications specified.
- Writing code that is well-designed and efficient.
- Analyzing, testing, and aiding with application integration.
- Performing software analysis.
- Application and software troubleshooting.
- Managing the development of applications.
- Assisting in the continuous enhancement of apps.
- Investigating and recommending technologies.
- Optimizing apps and systems.
- Identifying areas for improvement.
- Code optimization.
- Introducing new features.
- Assisting with software upgrades.

Bibliography

Akhin, M., & Belyaev, M. (n.d.). *Kotlin language specification*. Kotlin Language Specification; kotlinlang.org. Retrieved July 11, 2022, from https://kotlinlang.org/spec/introduction.html

Baeldung. (n.d.). *Kotlin*. Kotlin Java Interoperability. Retrieved July 11, 2022, from https://www.baeldung.com/kotlin/java-interoperability

Basic types | Kotlin. (2022, July 11). Kotlin Help; kotlinlang.org. https://kotlinlang.org/docs/basic-types.html

Collections overview | Kotlin. (2022, July 11). Kotlin Help; kotlinlang.org. https://kotlinlang.org/docs/collections-overview.html#collection-types

Comparator in Kotlin - GeeksforGeeks. (2019, July 30). GeeksforGeeks; www.geeksforgeeks.org. https://www.geeksforgeeks.org/comparator-in-kotlin/

Control Flow Statements in Kotlin. (n.d.). CherCherTech; chercher.tech. Retrieved July 11, 2022, from https://chercher.tech/kotlin/control-flow-kotlin

Dehghani, Ali. (n.d.). *Kotlin*. Operator Overloading in Kotlin. Retrieved July 11, 2022, from https://www.baeldung.com/kotlin/operator-overloading

Destructuring Declarations in Kotlin | raywenderlich.com. (n.d.). Destructuring Declarations in Kotlin | Raywenderlich.Com; www.raywenderlich.com. Retrieved July 11, 2022, from https://www.raywenderlich.com/22178807-destructuring-declarations-in-kotlin

EPS Software Corp., Wei-Meng Lee, C. M. (n.d.). *Introduction to Kotlin*. Introduction to Kotlin; www.codemag.com. Retrieved July 11, 2022, from https://www.codemag.com/Article/1907061/Introduction-to-Kotlin

Equality checks in Kotlin (Difference between "==" and "===" Operators). (n.d.). Equality Checks in Kotlin (Difference between "==" and "===" Operators); www.tutorialspoint.com. Retrieved July 11, 2022, from https://www.tutorialspoint.com/equality-checks-in-kotlin-difference-between-and-operators

Equality evaluation in Kotlin - GeeksforGeeks. (2019, August 2). GeeksforGeeks; www.geeksforgeeks.org. https://www.geeksforgeeks.org/equality-evaluation-in-kotlin/#:~:text=The%20referential%20equality%20in%20Kotlin,the%20same%20location%20in%20memory

Exceptions | Kotlin. (2022, July 11). Kotlin Help; kotlinlang.org. https://kotlinlang.org/docs/exceptions.html

Get started with Kotlin/Native in IntelliJ IDEA | Kotlin. (2022, July 11). Kotlin Help; kotlinlang.org. https://kotlinlang.org/docs/native-get-started.html

Heller, M. (n.d.). *What is Kotlin? The Java alternative explained | InfoWorld.* InfoWorld; www.infoworld.com. Retrieved July 11, 2022, from https://www.infoworld.com/article/3224868/what-is-kotlin-the-java-alternative-explained.html

Introduction to Kotlin - GeeksforGeeks. (2019, May 7). GeeksforGeeks; www.geeksforgeeks.org. https://www.geeksforgeeks.org/introduction-to-kotlin/

Is Kotlin the Future? - Source Technology. (2021, December 29). Source Technology; www.source-technology.com. https://www.source-technology.com/is-kotlin-the-future/#:~:text=The%20future%20is%20bright%20for%20Kotlin&text=This%20is%20because%20of%20many,having%20powerful%20and%20complex%20features

Kaseb, K. (2020, May 22). *Calling Java Codes from Kotlin. This essay aims to consider some... | by Kayvan Kaseb | Software Development | Medium.* Medium; medium.com. https://medium.com/kayvan-kaseb/calling-java-codes-from-kotlin-b74890fb4a78

Kotlin - Control Flow. (n.d.). Kotlin - Control Flow; www.tutorialspoint.com. Retrieved July 11, 2022, from https://www.tutorialspoint.com/kotlin/kotlin_control_flow.htm#:~:text=Kotlin%20flow%20control%20statements%20determine,do%20are%20flow%20control%20statements

Kotlin - Destructuring Declarations. (n.d.). Kotlin - Destructuring Declarations; www.tutorialspoint.com. Retrieved July 11, 2022, from https://www.tutorialspoint.com/kotlin/kotlin_destructuring_declarations.htm

Kotlin - Exception Handling. (n.d.). Kotlin - Exception Handling; www.tutorialspoint.com. Retrieved July 11, 2022, from https://www.tutorialspoint.com/kotlin/kotlin_exception_handling.htm

Kotlin - Override Method of Super Class. (n.d.). TutorialKart; www.tutorialkart.com. Retrieved July 11, 2022, from https://www.tutorialkart.com/kotlin/kotlin-override-method/

Kotlin Android Tutorial. (n.d.). TutorialKart; www.tutorialkart.com. Retrieved July 11, 2022, from https://www.tutorialkart.com/kotlin-android-tutorial/

Kotlin Array - javatpoint. (n.d.). Www.Javatpoint.Com; www.javatpoint.com. Retrieved July 11, 2022, from https://www.javatpoint.com/kotlin-array

Kotlin Class and Object - javatpoint. (n.d.). Www.Javatpoint.Com; www.javatpoint.com. Retrieved July 11, 2022, from https://www.javatpoint.com/kotlin-class-and-object

Kotlin Collections - Studytonight. (n.d.). Kotlin Collections - Studytonight; www.studytonight.com. Retrieved July 11, 2022, from https://www.studytonight.com/kotlin/kotlin-collections

Kotlin Control Flow - if else, for loop, while, range - JournalDev. (2018, February 4). JournalDev; www.journaldev.com. https://www.journaldev.com/18483/kotlin-control-flow-if-else-for-while-range

Kotlin Data Class. (n.d.). Kotlin Data Class; www.programiz.com. Retrieved July 11, 2022, from https://www.programiz.com/kotlin-programming/data-class

Kotlin Data Types. (n.d.). Kotlin Data Types; www.w3schools.com. Retrieved July 11, 2022, from https://www.w3schools.com/kotlin/kotlin_data_types.php

Kotlin Environment Setup IDE - javatpoint. (n.d.). Www.Javatpoint.Com; www. javatpoint.com. Retrieved July 11, 2022, from https://www.javatpoint.com/kotlin-environment-setup-ide

Kotlin Environment setup in Windows - bbminfo. (n.d.). Kotlin Environment Setup in Windows - Bbminfo; www.bbminfo.com. Retrieved July 11, 2022, from https://www.bbminfo.com/kotlin/kotlin-environment-setup.php

Kotlin Exception Handling | try, catch, throw and finally - GeeksforGeeks. (2019, June 25). GeeksforGeeks; www.geeksforgeeks.org. https://www.geeksforgeeks.org/kotlin-exception-handling-try-catch-throw-and-finally/

Kotlin For Android: An Introduction | raywenderlich.com. (n.d.). Kotlin For Android: An Introduction | Raywenderlich.Com; www.raywenderlich.com. Retrieved July 11, 2022, from https://www.raywenderlich.com/1144981-kotlin-for-android-an-introduction

Kotlin Hello World - You First Kotlin Program. (n.d.). Kotlin Hello World - You First Kotlin Program; www.programiz.com. Retrieved July 11, 2022, from https://www.programiz.com/kotlin-programming/hello-world

Kotlin Map - javatpoint. (n.d.). Www.Javatpoint.Com; www.javatpoint.com. Retrieved July 11, 2022, from https://www.javatpoint.com/kotlin-map

Kotlin Map : mapOf() - GeeksforGeeks. (2019, August 9). GeeksforGeeks; www.geeksforgeeks.org. https://www.geeksforgeeks.org/kotlin-map-mapof/

Kotlin Null Safety - Studytonight. (n.d.). Kotlin Null Safety - Studytonight; www.studytonight.com. Retrieved July 11, 2022, from https://www.studytonight.com/kotlin/kotlin-null-safety

Kotlin Operator Overloading - GeeksforGeeks. (2019, August 1). GeeksforGeeks; www.geeksforgeeks.org. https://www.geeksforgeeks.org/kotlin-operator-overloading/

Kotlin Regular Expression - GeeksforGeeks. (2019, July 9). GeeksforGeeks; www.geeksforgeeks.org. https://www.geeksforgeeks.org/kotlin-regular-expression/

Kotlin String Operations. (n.d.). TutorialKart; www.tutorialkart.com. Retrieved July 11, 2022, from https://www.tutorialkart.com/kotlin/kotlin-string-operations/

Kotlin Tutorial - javatpoint. (n.d.). Www.Javatpoint.Com; www.javatpoint.com. Retrieved July 11, 2022, from https://www.javatpoint.com/kotlin-tutorial

Miu, M. (2020, March 16). *Collections in Kotlin. The subject covered in this new post is... | by Magda Miu | ProAndroidDev*. Medium; proandroiddev.com. https://proandroiddev.com/collections-in-kotlin-a2bd8649f697

PACKT. (2019, January 24). *Interoperability between Java and Kotlin | Codementor*. Interoperability between Java and Kotlin | Codementor; www.codementor.io. https://www.codementor.io/@packt/interoperability-between-java-and-kotlin-rifmhfip0

Singh, C. (2019, March 8). *Kotlin Class and Objects - Object Oriented Programming (OOP)*. BeginnersBook; beginnersbook.com. https://beginnersbook.com/2019/03/kotlin-class-and-objects-oop/

Index

Printed in the United States
by Baker & Taylor Publisher Services

Printed in the United States
by Baker & Taylor Publisher Services